ENDORSEMENT

It has been a pleasure to know Bill Fitzgerald for over 20 years. Bill is a trusted leader in the career transition field, with extensive experience working with thousands of job seekers. His approach is pragmatic, refreshing and focused on achieving tangible results.

In *Searching for a Job Sucks*, Bill shares his results-driven methodology to demystify the increasingly complex job search process. Through actionable advice and real-life success stories, he equips readers with tools to navigate their job search with confidence and clarity. Here's what you'll gain from this book:

- How to clearly communicate your skills and career goals.

- Strategies for applying online that get you noticed.

- Effective use of LinkedIn and other platforms for research and targeting.

- Tips for crafting a resume that stands out.

- Networking techniques that lead to meaningful opportunities.

- Ways to manage unprepared and untrained interviewers.

- Insights into handling compensation discussions and knowing your worth.

Searching For A Job Sucks!

- Best practices for engaging with recruiters, Human Resources and hiring managers.

- How to determine the right cultural fit.

- Advice on how to use the latest technology.

- Guidance on how to effectively manage counteroffers.

Bill candidly addresses the harsh realities of job searching today, including age discrimination and all of the other obstacles job seekers face – all from the perspective of someone on the inside. He emphasizes that successful job searching is an active, strategic process that requires commitment and perseverance.

In summary, I highly recommend *Searching for a Job Sucks* to anyone considering or actively pursuing a new role. Bill's advice unlocks the secrets to navigating the job market and opens doors to exciting opportunities.

—Dale Klamfoth,
Founder and CEO, Careers in Business
Former Executive Director, Career Management Center, A. B.
Freeman School of Business at Tulane University
Former Senior Vice President, Lee Hecht Harrison

December 2024

"Practical advice, insights, and insider knowledge from the CEO of an executive search and recruiting firm."

SEARCHING FOR A JOB SUCKS!

An industry expert levels the playing field

BILL FITZGERALD

Searching For A Job Sucks!

Searching For A Job Sucks!

Copyright © 2025 by Bill Fitzgerald

International copyright laws protect this book. All rights reserved. Except for reviews, No part of this book may be reproduced, distributed, or transmitted in any form or by any means, including photocopying, recording, or other electronic or mechanical methods, without the prior written permission of the publisher, except in the case of brief quotations embodied in critical reviews and certain other noncommercial uses permitted by copyright law.

International Standard Book Number 979-8-30317190-9 Paperback

While the author has made every effort to provide accurate internet addresses at the time of publication, neither the publisher nor the author assumes any responsibility for errors or changes after publication. Further, the publisher has no control over and does not assume any responsibility for the author or third-party websites or their content. Some names, businesses, places, events, locales, incidents, and identifying details inside this book have been changed to protect the privacy of individuals.

Published and Printed in the United States of America by Fitzdrake Search Inc.

Cover and interior design: iamkerrywatson.com

Visit the author's website at www.billfitzgerald.biz

DEDICATION

To my friends Bob Benwick and Mike Keefe. You challenged and inspired me to be my best. I miss you both.

Searching For A Job Sucks!

TABLE OF CONTENTS

ENDORSEMENT i

DEDICATION v

A NOTE TO THE READER ix

CHAPTER 1: PREPARE 1

No One Cares Who You Are If You Can't Be Clear about What You Are . 1

You Can't Change Your Past, but You Can Create Your Future 13

10 Reasons Why You Shouldn't Change Jobs 22

6 to 8 Seconds Is All the Time You Have 26

LinkedIn Is Just a Database 51

Lessons from Job Seekers 59

    Finding a Job is a Job 59

    Everyone Can Be an A Player If They Are in the Right Role 62

    Look in the Mirror 66

CHAPTER 2: SEARCH 69

The Job Board Abyss 69

You Don't Pick a Search Firm; They Pick You 88

It's More Than Who You Know; It's All about Relationships 102

If You Are 50, You Are Now Considered Old 111

Lessons from Job Seekers 122

    Think Strategically 122

    Technology Isn't Always Your Friend 125

    Don't Run from Something; Run to Something 128

    You Don't Have to Apply for Everything 131

    What People Say and Think about You Matters 133

    The Fine Line Between Desperation and Interest 135

CHAPTER 3: INTERVIEW 139
Why You Get Hired 139
What's Below the Waterline? 168
HR Can Only Say "No" 179
Advice for Discouraged Job Seekers 185
What Comes after Rejection? 191
Lessons from Job Seekers 195
   Don't Get Caught Off Guard 195
   What Happens in Vegas…Doesn't Always Stay in Vegas 198
   Companies Only Care When They Are Hiring 203

CHAPTER 4: OFFER 205
Beware of Internal Equity 205
Buyer Beware 222
The New Boss 230
They Really Love Me—or Do They? 235
Lessons from Job Seekers 240
   There Is Always Something to Learn 240
   It's Okay to Say "No" 244
   Have a Plan 247

CHAPTER 5: LANDING 251
You've Landed, but It Begins Again 251
Lessons from Job Seekers 255
   Most People Want to Help—Karma Is a Boomerang 255
   Be Kind to Yourself 257
   Never Burn Bridges 262
   Never Assume a Job Is Forever 264

CHAPTER 6: 269
PUTTING IT ALTOGETHER 269
The Job Search Game Plan 269
Lessons from a Job Seeker 297

Don't Take This Trip Alone..297
CHAPTER 7: FINAL THOUGHTS..**301**
ABOUT THE AUTHOR...**307**
REFERENCES..**309**

A NOTE TO THE READER

I have been doing executive search and recruiting for the last 20 years. In that time, I have spoken to thousands of job seekers. While some are optimistic, most find the process discouraging, frustrating, and filled with disappointment. The emotional toll on one's self-confidence and self-esteem is hard to measure, but it's real. Finding a job is hard for most people. Many of those I speak to have no idea where to start. If they are unemployed and need to find a job, the process is even more challenging and scary. And, for people over 50 years old, finding a new job goes to another level of difficulty.

I wrote this book because I believe there is a job for everyone, and that working is central to our being. Work influences how we feel about ourselves and gives us a sense of worth. Work is how we leave our mark, make a difference for others, and care for those we love. It's often how we define ourselves and contribute to the greater good. I want everyone who wants a job, to find one. I wrote this book to make that possible and hopefully easier.

If you are looking for help with your job search, you've landed in the right place. I will share my insider's perspective and offer insights, advice, strategies and tactics so you can be more successful. I will tell you how recruiters and hiring managers think so you can compete on an even playing field. I also share stories from job seekers who have successfully landed in new roles and what they

Searching For A Job Sucks!

learned along the way. You may be doing a lot right, but with some fine-tuning, you may experience a needed breakthrough in your search.

Along the way, I also am brutally honest about what you are facing. The reason finding a job is so hard is because it is. The odds are stacked against you, and no one seems to care. Most of the recruiting and hiring products available in the marketplace are designed to help companies be more efficient. Companies are overloaded with resumes and applications and are looking for ways to screen you out before you ever get to speak with anyone. I'm sure you know the feeling of falling into a black hole. There are times when it seems like bots control the hiring process. That, combined with a general lack of common courtesy, makes job hunting, in too many cases, an awful experience.

I intend to cover every aspect of the job-searching process from writing a resume, job hunting, interviewing, networking and saying yes so you can be better prepared and know the best path to success. I will share everything I have learned to help you avoid the same mistakes, traps, and pitfalls. This book is your roadmap to making the job-seeking experience easier, and, hopefully, shorter. For the first time, maybe ever, you get a look behind the curtain so you can compete on a level playing field.

I have developed a number of resources for active and passive job seekers. You can learn more about them at https://billfitzgerald.biz.

All the best for a fruitful search.

—*Bill Fitzgerald* - *August 2024*

CHAPTER 1: PREPARE

No One Cares Who You Are If You Can't Be Clear about What You Are

I receive close to 100 unsolicited emails and resumes on a weekly basis. Who knows? One of them may have been yours! In most cases, I never click on the attachment. If I can't immediately tell in your email what you are or what makes you great, I immediately hit delete. If you are one of the lucky ones whose resume I open, you literally have a few seconds to answer that all-important question, and if you can't, I hit delete.

The resumes and cover letters that fail this first test are easy to spot. Some describe themselves with all the buzzwords and adjectives on the planet. They are good communicators, team players, collaborators, good listeners, influencers, innovators, strategic thinkers, player-coaches, and the lists go on and on. While these may be important skills, at this early stage of the process, I couldn't care less.

Others list so many areas of expertise I conclude they are probably mediocre at everything. Or, at the very least, confused about what they want to do next. You may have lots of experience, but you need to choose something that is easy to communicate, and more importantly, easy for the reader to grasp. If you list every possible role you could fill to avoid missing out, it is a self-fulfilling prophecy. The fear of missing out (FOMO) causes you to miss out.

I can promise you one thing for sure: if you can't be clear about what and who you are, I won't take the time to figure it out. If this sounds like you, stop applying for jobs and get off the playing field. If you are not experiencing success, this may be one reason why. You need to take a step back and get to know yourself better.

A successful job search begins with knowing what you want as an outcome. To know that you need to know yourself. If you don't know what you're great it, or what you love doing, or how you like to make a difference, or what you are trying to accomplish in your life, how can you possibly start looking for a job?

Unfortunately, people surge ahead, and ultimately, this leads to lots of frustration and disappointment. If you aren't clear, how can you expect a recruiter or hiring manager to figure it out? I can guarantee they won't. No one wants to own your confusion; not when other candidates are crystal clear.

So, What Do You Do?

I am not a trained career counselor, but I can recommend several resources you might find helpful. I have used these with many people, and I know they have found them helpful. All of these resources will get you thinking and help you find the focus you need when pursuing a new job.

Ikigai

If you haven't heard of *ikigai*, I suggest you check it out. Pronounced (ICK-ee-guy), it means "reason for being." In an InHerSight article, Ashley Alt described *ikigai* as "...your reason for jumping out of bed in the morning, what motivates you to revel in and appreciate life every day." Ikigai is the confluence of:

- What you love
- What you're good at
- What the world needs
- What you can be paid for

Think of ikigai as your sense of purpose or your reason for living.

Ikigai is meant to be a long-term practice, which is how you want to think about your career. You want to continually be asking yourself the following questions to find fulfillment in your career and your life. The questions are not intended to be a quick-fix solution and won't solve a mid-career crisis overnight. With time and continued meditation on the ikigai questions, you can discover the answers you are seeking.

Japanese culture suggests you meditate on the following four questions. While the questions are intended to apply to all aspects of your life, you can apply them to your career to find the direction you may be seeking.

Searching For A Job Sucks!

1. What do you love to do? Reflect on when you have been the happiest at work. What are you passionate about? Is there something at work that brings you absolute joy?

2. What am I good at? To answer this question, think about when and where you have had the greatest success, and when and what you have been recognized for. What contributions and accomplishments have been the most rewarding? In an article on People at Heart's website, "Find Your Ikigai," there is a helpful list of strengths you can use to identify what you are good at.

3. What does the world need? What is the higher purpose, calling, or underlining meaning to what you love to do and are good at? Ask yourself "why" something matters and after that, ask yourself again "why" that answer matters, and keep doing that after each answer until you find the true meaning and value of what you like to do. Think less about yourself and focus on how you can make a difference for others.

4. What can I get paid for? Bottom line: you need to make a living. If what you love, what you are good at, and what the world needs is useful, there may be a way to generate income.

My immediate reaction is to reach for a laptop or tablet and start capturing my answers to these questions. For many, it's going to feel like a brainstorm. You need to turn off the judging side of your brain and capture everything you can. However, don't force yourself to race through the questions to find an answer in one sitting. Allow enough time to reflect and think about each question.

I also think close friends and colleagues might have useful input on these questions. The people around you can tell when you are doing something you love and are good at, so don't be bashful and ask them. Provide them with some context and let them know you'll still be friends regardless of what they say. We can't be the best judge of ourselves, and this additional input—and that's all it is—can prove to be helpful.

Once you have gathered all of your input, it's time to review everything you have and look for themes that hopefully start to provide some direction. Your answers to these questions will be true for today, but you can expect them to change with age and experience. The idea is to keep asking and see what bubbles to the surface. This is all part of the career journey.

Myers Briggs

Another tool that can help with this discovery process is one I'm sure many people are familiar with, namely, the Myers Briggs Type Indicator (MBTI). The MBTI is a popular personality assessment tool based on the theories of Swiss psychiatrist Carl Jung. It is designed to help individuals better understand their preferences, behaviors, and decision-making processes. The MBTI categorizes individuals into one of 16 personality types based on four dichotomies:

Extraversion (E) or Introversion (I): Indicates whether individuals are energized by the external world and interactions (Extraversion) or by their inner thoughts and reflections (Introversion).

Searching For A Job Sucks!

Sensing (S) or Intuition (N): Represents how individuals gather information—through concrete facts and details (Sensing) or patterns, possibilities, and future implications (Intuition).

Thinking (T) or Feeling (F): Reflects how individuals make decisions—based on logic and objective analysis (Thinking) or on personal values and emotions (Feeling).

Judging (J) or Perceiving (P): Describes how individuals approach the outside world—in a structured, planned manner (Judging) or in a flexible, spontaneous way (Perceiving).

By identifying where individuals fall on each of these four dimensions, the MBTI generates a four-letter personality type, such as ISTJ or ENFP, which provides insights into their natural preferences and tendencies. The MBTI is commonly used in personal development, career counseling, team building, and relationship counseling to enhance self-awareness and interpersonal understanding.

You can find a detailed explanation of the 4 categories and the 16 personality types in a *Forbes* article written by Goldie Chan.

It's important to note that while the MBTI can offer valuable insights and facilitate self-discovery, it is not a definitive assessment of personality and should be used as a tool for reflection and growth rather than a strict categorization of individuals.

A free version of the Myers Briggs personality inventory is available at https://www.truity.com/test/type-finder-personality-test-new. The MBTI helps you filter and narrow down your choices. What you eliminate is often as valuable as what you want to explore further.

A companion to the inventory is a book titled *Do What You Are: Discover the Perfect Career for You Through the Secrets of Personality Type* (5th edition) by Barbara Barron, Paul Tieger, and Kelly Tieger. The authors lead readers step-by-step "through the process of determining and verifying personality type." From there, according to an Amazon review, "You'll learn which occupations are popular with each type, discover helpful case studies, and get a full rundown of your Type's work-related strengths and weaknesses." Another Amazon review claims, "Focusing on each type's strengths, *Do What You Are* uses workbook exercises to help readers customize their job search, get the most out of your current career, obtain leadership positions, and ensure that you achieve the best results in the shortest period."

The other value of the MBTI is what career alternatives it eliminates. This reduces the number you want to investigate and helps make deciding easier.

Values Card Sort

Another exercise that is both insightful and thought-provoking is the values card sort. I have used this in the past, and the answers provide a filter for evaluating all the different options you may be considering. It is referred to as the values card sort and its purpose is to help you prioritize and rank what you find most important regarding your life and career. The values card sort has been around for a long time and one I like is the "Knowdell Career Values Card Sorts." There is both an online and physical version. I prefer one that is more tactile and where you can work on a much bigger surface like a kitchen table. The online version is easier to share if that is what you prefer.

Searching For A Job Sucks!

The cards are not specific to any industry or discipline but are higher-level values associated with work that leads to happiness and satisfaction. This is a forced choice exercise that requires you to make trade-offs along the way. There is also a worksheet to evaluate your values against different career choices. At this moment in time, you'll know precisely what matters to you and be better positioned to make informed choices. The cost to purchase one set of cards is $20, which is very little when you consider the decisions you are trying to make. You can purchase the Knowdell Career Values Card Sorts at https://www.careerplanner.com/index.cfm.

Career Anchors

I have used Career Anchors for years and people who want to understand what drives them professionally find it very helpful. "Career anchors are the underlying drivers that make people feel fulfilled in their careers." Career Anchors does a wonderful job integrating external rewards, such as salary or prestige, and aligning those with internal motivations. According to the author, Edgar Schein, "each person has one dominant "anchor" that defines what they seek most in their work, influencing decisions such as job selection, career changes, and professional growth. Career Anchors is "a framework to help people better understand what motivates them in their professional lives so they make career decisions that reflect their personal priorities and lead to long-term fulfillment." The assessment is free and can be found at https://shorturl.at/4HUmy

The Assessment Warning Label

People sometimes believe that taking a career assessment will tell them exactly what they should do. That isn't the case and is why it's important to use several assessments in your career exploration. Assessment tools provide data points on many variables such as skills, interests, and personality. You need data on all three before drawing any definite conclusions. Even then, you want to consider life circumstances, market demand, and long-term career viability. I will also say that your interests and skills will evolve so what may be true today, may be very different in the future.

Career Coaching

If you are someone who needs to talk this out, and many are, the investment in a career coach might prove very useful. Sometimes the pain of getting laid off, the residual effects of a bad boss, lots of interviews and no offers or simply feeling stuck requires someone you can speak to confidentially and who can help you work through whatever is getting in your way—that's often you, but you can explore that more deeply in your next session. Marlo Lyons wrote an article for the *Harvard Business Review* titled "Do You Need a Career Coach?" in which she states that a career coach is "there to help you figure out what you want to do and understand assumptions you're making about yourself that are preventing you from advancing in your professional goals." What's not to like, right?

Here is an important caveat and it's a big one. Career coaches are not licensed, so anyone can call themselves a coach. In fact, becoming a coach seems very vogue these days. You need to do your research. Is this a full-time job? How much has the coach made in the last three years as a coach? At minimum, are they certified? The International Coach Federation is the gold standard certification, but for me, that isn't enough. Look for someone who has an M.S. or higher degree in counseling or a related field. In fact,

Searching For A Job Sucks!

if your medical provider has emotional health benefits, my recommendation is to check them out first and see if there is a provider who deals with career issues. Just because people call themselves "coaches" doesn't mean they are trained at the highest level or have the experience that can help you. Unless they have more advanced professional training, they are more like peer counselors.

Personally, I wouldn't trust your innermost gremlins to someone who isn't a highly trained and experienced professional. If you aren't sure what I mean by *gremlins*, check out *Taming Your Gremlin—A Guide to Enjoying Yourself* by Richard David Carson available on Amazon. My late friend, Bob Benwick, who held an M.S. in Organizational Development and was a Master Certified Coach and a former human resources executive, introduced me to this book. If you wrestle with doubt, a lack of confidence, or self-defeating beliefs, this book will help you move beyond whatever is holding you back. Whenever I feel stuck, I try to name the gremlin that is getting in my way so I can face it head-on.

I think the key to coaching is knowing what you need. If you need to learn how to change a tire, find someone who has changed thousands of tires and can teach you the best and safest way to change a tire. If you know how to change a tire, but lack the confidence, are frightened, or have images of a frustrated, impatient parent disappointed at your tire-changing performance, and you are frozen with indecision, find a mental health professional to help you with your stuff.

What's Next?

Armed with what you learn from the various assessments, now is the time to start looking for themes. What do you see over and over that looks interesting and appealing? What surprises do you see that require more thought? What possibilities does all this data start to illuminate that hold your attention? Revisit the answers to your *ikigai* and fine-tune your original thinking.

My recommendation is to start writing and describe the kind of role that sounds exciting. This isn't the professional summary you will show the world, so don't worry about length or even grammar. Just capture everything you can and create the story of you. Don't worry if you don't have an exact job title, but if you can, go for it!

In fact, once you have your story written, plug it into our new friend ChatGPT and ask what kind of jobs or job titles capture your interests, strengths, and desires. If you see ones that look intriguing, ask ChatGPT to tell you more about that job and ask what kind of people are attracted to a particular field. You can also read job postings to help you determine if a particular kind of work is what you'd like to do.

The Key Messages

Understanding your offer to the marketplace is the most critical question you need to answer when engaging in a job search. It doesn't matter if you are 25 or 65, establishing this level of clarity will transcend every aspect of your search and is needed to achieve a successful outcome.

Searching For A Job Sucks!

I can always tell the difference between those candidates who have done this work upfront and those who haven't. The ones who have, are very clear about who they are and what they offer. The others present a laundry list of possible options and expect me to believe they are great at everything. That is the most common mistake I see people make. You need to claim your area of expertise and run with it.

If you tend to rush past this chapter and keep reading, I strongly advise you to take some time to work through these exercises or others like them. As you will learn later, you only have seconds to make an introduction. I won't take the time to figure it out for you.

Once you think you've got, there is one other reality test I encourage you to try. Tell your close friends and colleagues what you are thinking and ask for their honest reaction and feedback. How they respond will tell you if you are ready to roll or have more work to do.

Coaching Questions

- If someone asks you what you are, can you tell them in one sentence?

- Is it crystal clear what makes you great?

- When people read your resume, will they know what you want to do next?

CHAPTER 1: PREPARE -No One Cares Who You Are If You Can't Be Clear about What You Are

You Can't Change Your Past, but You Can Create Your Future

As a recruiter, I interact with many job seekers whose careers are marked by many job changes. Maybe it's after a year, two years, or three years, but you rarely see sustained longevity in any organization or role. The constant change reminds me of playing checkers. People are constantly on the move and jumping from one organization to another. When someone's entire career history is marked by frequent changes, it raises a red flag for many hiring managers. It is also true for recruiters who need to understand the reasons for the changes and be able to explain them. Some stories are easier to tell than others, which is something you want to think about whenever you contemplate a change. How will you explain to a prospective employer when they ask you why you made a change, and a change after that, and so on? You better have a damn good story. It's one of the reasons you want to be strategic when managing your career.

There are times when those changes are outside of your control and that is understandable. The economy hits a downturn, new technology changes the way work is performed; restructuring or acquisitions occur, resulting in downsizing and layoffs; companies move or go out of business; or there is a once-in-a-lifetime pandemic. There are also times when the changes are voluntary. Whatever the reason, it is easy to get labeled a job hopper. Early in your career, more frequent job changes are common and even expected. We were all there at one time—trying to figure it out and finding the right path. If that pattern persists as you get older, it can create a significant challenge. While a hiring manager may admire ambition and courage, there is a potential downside you may not recognize until it is too late. Eventually, the lack of sustained success paints a less-than-positive impression and affects our ability to find a job—especially when you are unemployed. This is when the lack of longevity starts to become a challenge. I see this most often when the reason for leaving is involuntary and the person is over 50.

Sometimes, and this was certainly true in and around the pandemic, many people changed jobs to take advantage of a candidate-friendly market in order to make more money, get promoted, or even adjust how they worked—totally remote or hybrid. One had the sense that everyone was chasing the next shiny object, and it seemed like there was plenty to chase. There is a story here that many will understand. Unfortunately, as of this writing, the market has shifted back to an employer-friendly market, so if your career is marked by constant change, it gets harder to explain.

When someone has a history of short tenure, you can see it in the way they write their resume. You will read about responsibilities and lots of activity, but what you don't see are lots of results or quantifiable accomplishments. Why? For most jobs, it takes more than one year to generate sustainable change and improvement. It is easy to grab the low-hanging fruit and make a big splash. The real measure of success is how well you live with the consequences of your actions. Sticking around for the second or third act, seeing the longer-term impact of your work and what you've accomplished, correcting mistakes, and learning and continually improving are the real measures of success, and these take time. This is also how you learn and become more proficient at your craft. Short tenures limit the ability to develop and get smarter.

If I see a pattern of job hopping throughout someone's career, I think of them as a *C*-level player and someone I would present to only a small number of clients. I believe there is a home for everyone, but people with this kind of track record will have fewer options. This makes the job search process extremely difficult and requires a recalibration of where you look.

Just to be clear, when I'm talking longevity, I'm not describing the kind of longevity you might see among the silent generation (1925–1945) or some of the baby boomers (1946–1964). People in these generations, like my father, would spend 25 to 40 years working for the same company. For many reasons, those days have passed, and probably for good.

On the other hand, I agree with Chris Williams, a former Vice President of Human Resources (HR) at Microsoft, who wrote in a *Business Insider* article titled "How Long Is Too Long at One Job? How Short Is Too Short?" that "Younger recruiters look at an employee with 10 years at a company and ask what the problem was. Longer tenures have become their own red flag, and what was once seen as the minimum tenure now puts you in danger of being seen as a relic."

While there is no easy answer, I don't think about tenure as an absolute number so much as a trendline. What I like to see as you advance in your career are tenures that get to be longer. I'm talking about tenures that range between three to five to seven years, nothing unreasonable in my opinion. That number is based on my own experience, not scientific research. Others may argue longer or shorter, and for different roles, that may be true, but in my experience, you need that amount of time to make a sustainable impact. I understand I won't likely see that earlier in one's career. You need this time to try things out, to experiment, and to find your niche.

For me, tenure is a conversation that occurs simultaneously with accomplishments. I always look at what you contribute and how you make a difference. In many respects, that often matters more. I'm looking for people who get things done and make an impact. However, companies are reluctant to invest in people who bounce too frequently, so you need to find a balance.

There is another reason this is so important, and it doesn't show up until later in your career, when you are around 50 years old. Consider this a warning to the younger generation. Emily Brandon wrote "7 Tips for Getting Hired After Age 50" for *U.S. News & World Report* and cited that "Once out of work, older workers seem to have greater difficulties landing a new position. The average duration of unemployment for job seekers ages 55 to 64 was 20.9 weeks in March 2020, compared with an average of 17.5 weeks of unemployment among all workers, according to an AARP (formerly the American Association of Retired Persons) Public Policy Institute analysis of Bureau of Labor Statistics data."

While age discrimination likely plays a role here, many of the older adults I deal with have backgrounds that have one thing in common; their backgrounds are full of short tenures. Saying what I am about to say won't make me many friends, but it is too easy and convenient to blame age discrimination as the reason for not finding a job. Some of this is not the result of age.

There is another downside to these short tenures and that is the inability to build a strong network. I find that people with short tenure have difficulty finding a job via networking. They either don't have the relationships or people are reluctant to recommend them. With 80% of professional-level jobs found via networking, this creates a significant disadvantage. When I talk to these folks about networking, they, without hesitation, tell me they don't know anyone or don't have a network. While I know that isn't true and can help them think through who they do know, these individuals start their job search in a deficit position.

To pull on this further, many recruiters have different ways to categorize candidates. Some use a simple *A*, *B*, and *C* system. Your top talent falls in bucket *A*, good to very good talent falls in bucket *B*, and everyone else, whom they will likely never call, falls in bucket *C*. If you are someone whose career is marked by the following issues described, you will fall in bucket *C*.

So, What Can You Do?

Think strategically about your career. Make sure your decisions and actions align with your longer-term objectives. I understand objectives may change over time, which leads to unforeseen changes but those are easy stories to tell.

When a recruiter reviews your resume, whether consciously or unconsciously, they are placing you in one of several buckets. That initial categorization is determined by your overall career history.

Searching For A Job Sucks!

This helps a recruiter or hiring manager determine if this company or role is the right fit. The idea here is to think strategically about your career and make sure your decisions and actions align with your longer-term objective. I understand that objectives may change over time, which leads to unforeseen changes but those are easy stories to tell.

Here is my best strategic advice:

- Work for the most well-known, highly respected brands, big or small, as you can. The assumption is that you get exposed to more advanced practices, processes, and talented people, and ultimately, learn more.

- Be conscious of tenure and the impact it has on your career. As Chris Williams wrote in his *Business Insider* article, "Job hopping can be seen as a sign of restlessness, immaturity, and an inability to stick through the tough times." Understand the story you can tell a prospective employer. Does it pass the smell test?

- Focus on significant and measurable accomplishments. Recruiters and hiring managers are looking for people who can demonstrate an impact on the business. Being busy with lots of activity doesn't impress anyone.

- Focus on progression. Progression doesn't always have to mean vertical; it can also mean horizontal by becoming more expert in your chosen field.

- Build relationships and maintain those most critical relationships. Not only will these people help you succeed in

CHAPTER 1: PREPARE - No One Cares Who You Are If You Can't Be Clear about What You Are

your current job, but they will very likely help you find your next job. You can't succeed without help from others. Be seen as someone who regularly pays it forward.

- If you change jobs involuntarily, be honest and upfront about the circumstance while not blaming others. Own it and move forward.

- Ensure you have a resume that clearly and concisely communicates what you are, where you have done it, and what you have accomplished.

We can't work for the most well-known and most successful companies in the world. Our experience, education, personality, and so on will never make that possible. What you can do, is aspire to the best organizations possible. Implied here are names and brands, for-profit and non-profit, that other people will recognize. These organizations have outstanding records of success and strong brand name recognition. Those are the experiences, with adequate tenure and accomplishments, that will help sustain your career and help you climb the career ladder as high as you can or would like to go.

Success isn't always defined as vertical. It can be equally rewarding and successful to work horizontally.

I don't believe anyone should feel embarrassed or disappointed if they find themselves working for an AA organization if they are doing well and feel satisfied. In the course of your career, it's important to recognize where you fit best. The hope is that everyone earns a good living, experiences as much professional success as possible, and achieves a high degree of personal satisfaction. You don't have to play in the major leagues for that to happen. For some organizations where you are the perfect fit, you might actually be an *A*-level candidate. It's all relative.

Just like recruiters are looking for the best fit, you too need to achieve a level of self-awareness and acceptance to find the right fit. Don't fall into the trap of continually changing jobs looking for the proverbial gold ring you may already have. That's important to understand because continually changing jobs, but not advancing to the next level, forms a pattern that raises red flags when a recruiter looks at your resume.

Remaining in a job, any job, long enough to show meaningful and sustainable contributions not only generates satisfaction but opens the door to other opportunities if that's what you want for yourself.

Key Messages

While we talk a lot about tenure and why it matters, staying in a job long enough to make meaningful and sustainable contributions is how you will advance in your career. Smart hiring managers look for people who are ambitious, talented, and able to solve their problems. Focus on what you can accomplish and how you can make a lasting difference. This leads to greater job satisfaction and opens the door to other opportunities if that's what you want for yourself.

Be mindful of making frequent job changes just to do the same job over at another organization.

Eventually, you will find yourself stuck. If this sounds like you, it's time to focus on what you do well and settle down. Depending on your age, you may also need to recalibrate your expectations. For anyone earlier in their career, be mindful when you make changes. Make them for the right reasons and think longer term.

Ultimately it comes down to finding the right fit where you can be happy and successful. If you are willing to look around, there may be more opportunities for growth and development in your current organization than you realize.

Coaching Questions

- How do you define career happiness and satisfaction?
- If you are considering a change, what will be different, what will you learn, and how does it move you toward your ultimate goal?
- What's the story you can tell others about why you are changing jobs?

Searching For A Job Sucks!

10 Reasons Why You Shouldn't Change Jobs

This might seem like an unusual topic to cover in a book about job hunting. However, I believe it's worth introducing. Changing jobs isn't easy, professionally or personally. Aside from the time, effort, and disruption, there is a lot of uncertainty and risk. We have all seen examples where changing jobs hasn't been the answer. You may even know that from firsthand experience.

As someone who makes a living helping people explore new jobs, you would expect me to tell you that now is the perfect time to make a change. Your willingness to consider new opportunities certainly makes my job easier. However, as someone who cares more about your long-term career success, I'd rather give you some reasons why it might make sense to stay where you are, at least for the time being.

So, What Can You Do?

- Be sure you have been in your current job long enough to make meaningful, substantial contributions. Accomplishments are the currency on which you build a career and without them, it is hard to move up and advance as opposed to making lots of lateral moves. I like to work with candidates who have been in their current job at least two to three years. That is usually enough time to tackle more than just the low-hanging fruit. I want people who know how to work through the hard stuff and can make a difference that sticks.

- Assess if you are still learning and feeling challenged. Your career success reflects how much and how quickly you can learn. You always want to be learning and getting smarter. Don't walk away if you can continue to add to your portfolio of knowledge, skills, and abilities.

- Be honest about your boss. Are they someone who actually care about your success and is a good coach and advocate? It is often said that people rarely leave their jobs; they leave their boss. If you are fortunate and have a boss who actually cares about your success, don't take that for granted.

- Ask yourself if you feel fairly paid for your level of experience and what you contribute. You can almost always make more money elsewhere. That is how the market works. What you are paid is only one aspect of job satisfaction. Just be aware of the trade-offs when someone offers you a few more shekels.

- Do you enjoy the people you work with and find yourself getting better and smarter from the association? More than likely, you spend more time with the people at work than you do your own family or dog or cat or whatever keeps you company evenings and weekends. Don't underestimate the value of these relationships. They can pay dividends for many years.

- Think about the day-to-day and if you still enjoy what you do and are having fun. If you are excited to go to work most days and don't resent the extra time and effort required to do all it takes to succeed, don't take your happiness for granted.

Searching For A Job Sucks!

- Make sure your job provides the flexibility you need to take care of other priorities in your life—raising children, attending to elderly parents, volunteering, a hobby, and so on.

- Identify realistic possible opportunities for advancement and career progression. Find out what opportunities might exist and possible time frames. Take the initiative to pursue possible moves that might contribute to your career success and happiness.

- If you commit to finding a new job, prepare yourself for lots of work and marshal the emotional energy it will take. Seriously, if you aren't ready to put in the effort, don't waste your time. Finding a new job is often like another full-time job, so realize what you are getting into and ask yourself if it's worth the effort.

- Determine if your current organization is financially strong and moving in a direction you find exciting. If you continue to perform well, this can potentially mean more opportunities.

Key Messages

Ultimately, it is important to remember that you are more than just your job; career decisions should never be made in a vacuum. If you are happy with the quality of your life and can spend time where you want to spend it, you may be exactly where you need to be.

If you decide to make a change, be clear about what's missing in your current job. Go beyond a "feeling" and put a "name" to what's missing and what needs to be different.

Before you venture out, explore and take advantage of everything your current organization has to offer. There may be more opportunities there than you realize.

Finally, if you decide to look, commit yourself to the time and effort needed to navigate a successful job search. You can't look for a job halfway and expect a successful outcome.

Coaching Questions

- How do you contribute to your own dissatisfaction and how you could make the situation better?

- How will changing jobs affect your life outside of work?

- What is missing in your current job and what would make it better?

Searching For A Job Sucks!

6 to 8 Seconds Is All the Time You Have

Over the years, I have read thousands and thousands of resumes. Despite all the books, articles, videos, webinars, and other media on how to write a good resume, why are so many so bad? If you are writing a resume, you need to realize your resume is often the only introduction you may get to the reader. You won't get a second chance. Most recruiters and hiring managers are so busy if they can't quickly see a good match, they won't give your resume a second look. While you may spend hours writing what you think is the perfect characterization of your life history, you'd be shocked and disappointed at how little time people spend reading your masterpiece.

In a November 2022 article for StandOut CV titled "How Long Do Recruiters Spend Looking at Your Resume?", Andrew Fennell reported, "Recruiters spend 6 to 8 seconds reviewing a resume before they decide whether it's suitable for a vacancy or not." He also said, "80% of resumes do not get short-listed by recruiters, meaning they don't make it past the first screen." In other words, you don't have much time to make a positive first impression.

How many hours, and in some cases, how much money have you spent hand-crafting this document so it can be dismissed in a matter of seconds? If you can't pass this first test, it is an absolute waste of time and money.

As a job seeker, you need to understand why.

First, many resumes get submitted by job seekers who aren't even remotely qualified for the job they have applied for. This is a waste of time for everyone. In the same article previously mentioned, Andrew stated that "on average only 11% of applicants are considered suitable for the roles they are applying in." Stop clicking the LinkedIn "Easy Apply" button and wondering why no one has called you back. Your resume is buried deep in a database and will never be heard of again.

Another reason, and I know you will find this hard to believe, is that your resume isn't the strongest one in the bunch. I know, you think you are totally qualified and a perfect fit, but that's not for you to judge.

It is also possible that your resume is so poorly written that no one has taken it seriously. When you submit your resume for a job, you only get one shot to get it right. That's why you need to make it easy for the reader to read so they can quickly understand what you are, where you have worked, what you are responsible for, and what you have accomplished. Recruiters won't take the time to figure this out.

You also need to understand that recruiters have a huge bias around resume format. Most of my recruiting colleagues, including myself, absolutely can't stand the functional resume. Wading through a long list of accomplishments without context is virtually meaningless. Do you expect the reader to call upon some higher power to discern where and when each accomplishment occurred? I guarantee that won't happen. I understand a functional resume is a way to conceal information like gaps in employment or a lack of experience, but I will eventually figure that out. And when I do, I will be so annoyed that you wasted my time you will be rejected and banished to a planet in the Outer Rim.

Searching For A Job Sucks!

The other thing that makes me crazy is when people include a long list of skills on their resume right below their professional summary or at the top. I know why they are doing it—they want an applicant tracking system (ATS) algorithm to find them when a recruiter is searching. However, the skills are often so generic that the list is borderline useless, and for me, annoying. For example, don't tell me you are a team player, detail-oriented, self-starter, good listener, collaborator, and so on. I would love someone to put on their resume that they don't get along with others, are highly inflexible, and only do the bare minimum. That would mean something! If you can list technical skills like programming languages, relevant technical tools, or specific functional expertise, that's likely to get my attention.

Place this list at the bottom of your resume so it gets found by a search engine. You want the recruiter to see what you are, where you have been working, and what you have accomplished as quickly as possible. If you want people to know you are a team player or have good communication skills, capture that in one of your accomplishments.

So, What Can You Do?

Lindsay Kolowich Cox wrote an updated article (August 25, 2017) titled "21 Things Recruiters Absolutely Hate about Your Resume." I've captured many of Lindsay's points in the following. I have also added and expanded on some.

While this may sound like Resume 101 I am often shocked by what I see.

- If you use Google Docs before sending, save your resume as a PDF to preserve the formatting. If you share your resume as a Google Doc, grant proper permissions.

- If you use Hotmail, Yahoo, or AOL email addresses, you date yourself.

- Don't get cute with your fonts unless you are in a field that values creativity. The most common font is Times New Roman in 12-point in size. Only use one font in your resume.

- Do you think anyone cares where you went to high school?

- Listing your GPA is okay if you are a new graduate, but after you starting working, no one cares except your parents.

- If you have multiple degrees and list GPA, do it for both.

- Don't list technology you know unless you are an expert. I know Excel, but I don't know how to run pivot tables or how to set up Complex formulas.

- Keep your formatting the same throughout the resume. Maintain even margins and align items properly.

- Don't use pronouns *I* or *my* or *we*.

- Make sure your verb tenses are in the past except for your current position.

Searching For A Job Sucks!

- Avoid large chunks of text—bullets are the key to being read. Remember, you have 6 to 8 seconds to make your case.

- Ensure adequate white space. Don't make this an eye test. Remember, professionals get judged by their ability to discern what's most important. Just because it sticks doesn't mean it belongs on your resume.

- Eliminate annoying jargon and business buzzwords, and replace those with clear statements about what you did.

- Explain your gaps. If there is anything that raises a red flag for a recruiter it is gaps in your employment history. You need to explain those gaps and be honest. Examples include time with family, a sabbatical, travel, and a coma.

- Make sure your resume is consistent with your LinkedIn profile. Recruiters and hiring managers will look for inconsistency, which raises a red flag.

- When you send your resume with an email, write an email that is clear and concise.

I would add the following to this list:

- Irrelevant hobbies and interests—I don't care if you are into quilting, gardening, or bike riding. I want to know if you can do this job—not how you spend your free time.

- Your grammar matters, and so do misspellings. I know recruiters who will eliminate a resume even for a minor typo. Remember, the resume you are competing against is perfect.

- A professional headshot—why would you do this unless you want to be an actor? Why would you intentionally invite unconscious bias? Most people are not that good-looking, so why draw unnecessary attention?

- I believe it's important to have a summary statement at the top, but most of what I see doesn't answer the most important questions: "What are you?" If I read your summary and all I learn is that you are a team player with good interpersonal skills who works well cross-functionally and is well liked and respected by their peers, I'm ready to puke on my shoes.

- Leave the details for jobs 20 years or older off your resume. While I agree you want to dive deep into your most recent and relevant experiences, it's important to reference what you did early in your career. You won't include anything more than the title, company, and years you worked there, but the information is essential to complete the entire picture.

- People often ask me a lot about the appropriate length for a resume. In this digital age, I don't think it matters that much. However, not long ago, I had an executive send me his resume, and it wasn't until I printed his document that I realized it was 10 pages long! The fact that an executive gave me a 10-page resume immediately disqualified him for the job. Even the most experienced professional needs to fit everything between two to four pages. Anything more than that, and I stop reading.

- It's more important than ever to include your address. If I am only looking for local candidates, I don't want to waste my time with someone looking for a remote opportunity. Also, if you are only open to remote or hybrid roles, say so, and we won't waste time.

- One of the most important points has to do with the actual content. It is imperative to understand the distinction between responsibilities and accomplishments, and I'll dive into that later in the chapter.

The other trend I'm seeing is what I call form over substance. So many resumes seem to be written by professional resume designers and writers biased toward graphs, charts, color, and many words. I'm talking dense paragraphs of words that include every buzzword they can squeeze into the document.

Here is the problem—the writers have completely forgotten what matters to the reader. The fluff and artsy-fartsy stuff is just annoying. Sure, a resume must be visually appealing, but that has more to do with white space, font size, and using bullets. What I see now has gone way over the top—to the point where some resumes are too painful to read.

Here is some advice you can take to the bank: write a resume that people will read. Now that's a blinding statement of the obvious, right? So, what is the secret? Stop thinking about writing a resume and think more about interviewing. Start writing your resume by

CHAPTER 1: PREPARE -No One Cares Who You Are If You Can't Be Clear about What You Are

working backward. Writing a resume isn't easy, but the task becomes much easier if you think more about preparing for an interview and what readers want to see.

There are four questions an interviewer is attempting to answer:

1. What are you?

2. Where have you worked?

3. What have you been responsible for?

4. What have you accomplished?

These are the four questions I attempt to answer when I read a resume. It also represents the roadmap my eyes follow when I read a resume. Everything else is noise and a distraction.

What Are You?

The first question you often get asked in an interview is, "Tell me about yourself." Interviewers use this question to determine your professional identity. The answer to this question is your professional summary, which must be at the top of your resume. Most importantly it is a statement unique to you and what makes you special professionally.

The professional summary statement needs to be clear and concise. It should not bore readers with a statement that thousands of others could write about themselves. It should be unique, one that you alone can claim. If you did the work recommended at the beginning of the book, you should have enough information to generate a compelling statement.

Searching For A Job Sucks!

What about your area of functional expertise, industry specialization, and years of experience? For example:

I am an accomplished entrepreneur/investor/business owner in the DC Metro area. I have worked in the HR/OD space for 30 years.

What makes you unique speaks to your expertise; the more specific, the better. For example:

With expertise in Executive Search, Recruiting, and Organizational Development, I've worked with start-ups and Fortune 500 organizations in multiple industries, including HR Outsourcing, Manufacturing, Food, and the Internet.

What do you want to do tells the reader immediately if there might be a fit. For example:

Seeking a senior-level talent acquisition role in a mid-sized technology company.

In a matter of seconds, the reader knows enough about you to know if it makes sense to keep reading. The key is to be as specific and relevant as possible. Does this mean you get passed over for other opportunities you find interesting? Absolutely! Sometimes, you aren't the right fit, and no one will hire you only because you are interested. That is also why you must tailor your professional summary each time you submit a resume. You may also need to choose different accomplishments to highlight other skills. One size will never fit all, but we can always present ourselves differently, highlighting various aspects of our background in a way that makes sense to the reader. That's why blasting out hundreds of resumes will likely be a waste of time. I believe less is more; the more targeted, the more customized you can be with your messaging, the better.

Some people keep their professional summaries general because they fear being too specific and missing a possible opportunity. They expect the reader to figure it out. I hate to be the bearer of bad news —that isn't going to happen. No one wants to own your confusion and trying to be everything to everyone so you don't miss a possible opportunity is how you miss every opportunity.

Here is how I test someone's summary statement. If I can scratch out the author's name and insert almost any other name in its place, it's a waste of my time to read. It's also a waste of time for someone to write.

You need to clearly and concisely tell us about your specific value in the marketplace and how you would like to apply that value. Think about the following questions to get you thinking:

- What are you?
- What are you great at?
- What makes you stand out?
- What is your offer to the marketplace?
- Where can you make your most significant contribution?

The answers to these questions will help you write a more specific, focused, and personal statement.

Searching For A Job Sucks!

Here are some examples so you can see what I mean:

- Over two decades of expertise in Global HR Operations (HRSS), HR Technology/Digital transformation, and global HR Analytics & Data governance. Worked with C-suite executive leadership across seven continents to build and implement people strategies, set up global HR Functions and COEs, and transform HR Functions into digital/data-driven and innovative service delivery functions. Seeking a director-level role to lead HR analytics and transformation.

- Highly effective global business operations executive with diverse experience spanning industries, including Management & Strategy Consulting, Financial Services, and Human Capital Management. Deep expertise in operations, business process outsourcing, contract negotiations, vendor management, major project & program management, business development, and strategic partnering. Global experience in the EU, UK, India, Australia, and multiple areas of the United States. Seeking an opportunity to lead a small to midsized technology company.

- Accomplished salesperson with three years of experience selling enterprise hardware and software products and services to large corporate clients. Seeking an opportunity to apply my ability to prospect, engage, present, and close new business in the sports marketing environment.

Artificial intelligence (AI) can also help you write your summary statement. Take, for example, the preceding summary statements. If I plug that into ChatGPT, the first thing it does is tell me what I'm seeking and where there is alignment between my background and career aspirations. Ask yourself, does that make sense? Is that really what I want? If not, go back to the previous five questions and give them more thought.

If you ask ChatGPT to rewrite your summary statement, it sounds like the following:

As a seasoned entrepreneur, investor, and business owner based in the DC Metro area, I bring over three decades of experience in the HR/OD field. Specializing in Executive Search, Recruiting, and Organizational Development, I have collaborated with a spectrum of companies, from start-ups to Fortune 500 enterprises, across diverse sectors such as HR Outsourcing, Manufacturing, Food, and the Internet. Currently aiming to transition into a senior-level talent acquisition position within a mid-sized technology firm.

ChatGPT can bring a level of clarity and sophistication to your writing. More than likely, you'll want to remove some words to keep the statement as concise as possible. For example, you can say:

Seasoned entrepreneur, investor, and business owner based in the DC Metro area, with over three decades of experience in the HR/OD field. Specializing in Executive Search, Recruiting, and Organizational Development. Experience in start-ups to Fortune 500 enterprises, across diverse sectors such as HR Outsourcing, Manufacturing, Food, and the Internet. Searching for a senior-level talent acquisition position within a mid-sized technology firm.

Remember, this is where my eyes go first so I want to see a statement that is clear and concise without lots of filler words. So, while ChatGPT can be very helpful, don't forget to apply the filters discussed earlier.

Searching For A Job Sucks!

Where Have You Worked?

Next, we are into the meat of the resume that most readers care about. What you include here determines if your resume merits further examination. Your goal is to give them enough targeted content to catch their attention. It all begins with how you present your experience.

It's common for an interviewer to review your background and ask what was significant about each role. To answer this question, you need to indicate on your resume where you have worked, what your roles are, and for how long.

For your most recent job and the previous 20 years, if you have that much experience, you will list the organization and how long you worked there. Below the organization's name, you need to include two or three sentences about the organization, often in italics. You can't assume the reader will know anything about Joe's Rag Shop. Indicate if the company is public or private, its industry, product or service, annual revenue, and the number of employees.

What follows is a statement that starts with "Responsible for." It is critical here to distinguish between responsibilities and accomplishments. Responsibilities describe the scope of your job. Included are your primary accountabilities, team size, budget responsibility, and so on. You provide the reader with a sense of scope.

Here are a few examples:

Responsible for leading the firm's strategic direction to improve overall business efficiency and develop a scalable growth model. Directly leads finance, sales and marketing, information technology, human resources, and operations support across the firm.

Responsible for providing business analysis and systems configuration expertise while working across multiple projects to support Joe's Rag Shop's mission to become an information technology company that also sells insurance. Served as a team leader, responsible for supervising process organization, job code management, and staff training.

Responsible for growing market share through new account acquisition and existing account progression in NC/SC/GA.

Responsible for the employee experience and leveraging the company's competitive compensation and benefits structures to recruit and retain top talent. Direct report to the CEO, 325 HR employee function, Advisor to senior execs and BOD, $300M HR Budget,

Responsible for the Iowa territory at Joe's Rag Shop, working with enterprise customers primarily in the western half of Iowa. Ran a business book business with over 70 customers, primarily in manufacturing. Worked as an extension of the client's IT team, providing proper technical resources to deliver their equipment and software on time.

Searching For A Job Sucks!

Responsible for leading Joe's Rag Shop dental, life, disability, vision, and workers' compensation businesses that cover 10M members, generate $1.5B in revenue, and include 1,800 associates.

Responsible for leading Anthem's dental, life, disability, vision, and workers' compensation businesses, which cover 15M members, generate $1.2B in revenue, and include 1,200 associates.

Each statement is clear, concise, and specific to the writer. They are based more on functional, technical, or industry expertise, making it easy for the reader to understand who they are meeting on paper.

What Have You Accomplished?

Next, the interviewer will ask about accomplishments, what you are most proud of, where you have made the most significant contribution, and so on. What follows is a statement that starts with "Accomplishments include" or "Contribution includes" and then bullet, bullet, bullet.

The reader is looking for measurable outcomes, contributions, and results as much as possible. The more you can quantify these statements, the better. I recently had a candidate submit a resume that looked like she cut and pasted her human resources (HR) job description into her resume. There was no mention of accomplishments, just a long list of responsibilities and activities. Ask yourself what kind of results the reader will care about.

It is best to use bullet points to describe accomplishments. That makes them easier to read. I also like them under the job where they occurred, so I have adequate context.

I am adamant about this focus on outcomes for many reasons, and a client reminded me last week why it matters. After reading a candidate's resume, she commented on the number of "activities" versus "results," which concerned her.

Her comment was a great reminder of what truly matters to a hiring manager. If your resume doesn't clearly distinguish between "responsibilities" and "accomplishments," you risk communicating the wrong message to the reader. If your resume is nothing more than a long list of activities and responsibilities, the reader will question your approach to work. In other words:

- Do you understand the language of business?

- Do they know how to make a sustainable difference, and the effort that's required?

- Do you understand your organization's priorities?

- Do you understand the difference between *activities* and *outcomes*?

A potential employer wants to see accomplishments or outcomes that reflect meaningful results. Here is a simple test. After each activity you have listed on your resume, repeatedly ask yourself, "Why does it matter?" until you discover why something matters. Everything may not be easily measured, but the goal is to get as close as possible to how you made a difference that mattered to an external or internal customer. How have you influenced cost, quality, timeliness, or service? That's the kind of person an employer wants to hire!

Searching For A Job Sucks!

The accomplishments you include on your resume may be customized depending on the job.

Here are a few examples:

- Started with a book goal of approximately 50K per month and raised that to a goal of over 200K monthly.

- Enhanced IT system security, stability, and efficiencies, achieving and maintaining critical operational system uptime of 99.99%.

- One of only 33 salespeople (out of 180) to exceed budget in all five major product categories in 2 consecutive years.

- Boosted attendance at the annual summit series by 400% and sponsorship revenue by 50% through the launch of live-streamed events, video interviews, etc.

- Successfully implemented the Workday Cloud solution within the required 12-month implementation plan.

- Restructured the finance team to drive strategic initiatives across the firm. Implemented a new billing and invoicing system to create a centralized function within finance. This improved efficiency and standardization, reducing our accounts receivable by over 40% while increasing client consistency.

I love that these examples speak the language that a hiring manager cares about—results. Each statement begins with an action word that leads to an outcome. How you accomplished those results matters, but that comes later in the interview.

Writing accomplishments is also the time to demonstrate the soft skills that matter to the organization. Place items like teamwork, collaboration, problem-solving, and so on in the context of getting something done that genuinely matters.

After your work history, you can list awards, technical skills, conference presentations, volunteer experience, and anything relevant to the reader.

Education is probably last on your resume. If someone has more than three years of experience, the education goes at the bottom before listing any certifications, licensures, and so on. Less than five years of education can be noted at the top, before work history.

Start with the highest degree earned first and where you went to school. You also need to include the years attended. Including the dates you attended school is just part of telling your story. If you didn't graduate, indicate the school and years attended.

Finally, I still see resumes that reference their marital status and children. I don't care for legal reasons; otherwise, I'm not interested.

See the following resume outline to get a visual idea of what this looks like. This outline is ideal for any professional two-plus years out of school.

Searching For A Job Sucks!

Name
City, State * Phone * Email * LinkedIn Profile

Professional Summary

Professional Experience

Name of Organization- City/State   **Month/Year to Present**
Company description – in italics.

Title   **Month/Year to Present**
Responsible for….
Key Accomplishments
-
-
-

Title   **Month/Year to Month/Year**
Responsible for….
Key Accomplishments
-
-
-

Title   **Month/Year to Month/Year**
Responsible for….
Key Accomplishments
-
-
-

Name of Organization – City/State   **Month/Year to Present**
Company description – in italics.

Title   **Month/Year to Present**

Responsible for….

Key Accomplishments
-
-
-
-

Title   **Month/Year to Present**

Responsible for….

Key Accomplishments
-
-
-
-

Any company you worked over 20 years ago:
Name of Company – City/State
Title

Name of Company – City/State
Title

Name of Company – City/State
Title

Education

Degree, Name of School, city, state
Degree, Name of School, city, state

Certifications

Use bullets to list the most job-related certifications.

Awards

Searching For A Job Sucks!

Use bullets to list the most relevant awards.

Community and Volunteer Experience

Use bullet points to list community and volunteer experience.

Skills

Use bullet points to list the most relevant technical or functional skills.

Language

Languages you speak other than your native language

Here is another version that is ideal for someone coming out of school or looking for an internship. It is very similar with several noticeable differences.

First, your professional summary should read more like an objective statement that outlines what you'd like to do. Also, you should include your education upfront, so the reader sees the connection between your objective and education. You want to include work experiences, internships' demonstrating your willingness to work hard and take initiative.

Full Name
City, State * Phone * Email* LinkedIn Profile

OBJECTIVE

This statement describes what you'd like to do. For example, to obtain an internship that will broaden my understanding of ABC.

Or

To obtain an entry-level position as a software developer applying my front end programming skills in HTM, CSS and JavaScript

EDUCATION

Name of school, city, and state
Expected date of graduation: month and year
School or department:
Major and minor:
Current GPA:
Other academic experiences such as studying abroad

WORK EXPERIENCE

Title   **Month/Year to Present**
Responsible for....
Key Accomplishments
-
-
-
-

Title   **Month/Year to Present**
Responsible for....

Key Accomplishments
-
-
-
-

Title   **Month/Year to Present**
Responsible for....
Key Accomplishments
-
-
-
-

Searching For A Job Sucks!

CERTIFICATIONS
Any work-related training/professional development

EXTRACURRICULAR ACTIVITIES
Activities and volunteer experience

SKILLS
Technical/functional skills you'd like to highlight

Both examples are easy to read, which is what I like about them. That needs to be your primary focus when developing a resume. The message here is to keep it simple. That is what your reader wants to see, so don't screen yourself out by making it overly complicated.

Here is another piece of insight you might find helpful. When I look at a resume, my eyes start at the top, and I review the professional summary to determine whether the person I'm about to meet on paper is the right person. Next, my eyes look at the left-hand side of the document, and I want to see where someone has worked. I then go back and look at their responsibilities and accomplishments. You've lost your opportunity if you make me work too hard to figure any of this out. If I like what I see, I will put it in the pile—digital or otherwise—to review later. If not, listen for that flushing sound.

You'll notice there are no graphics. To me, graphics, headshots, and so on, are a distraction and a red flag that tells me there is a resume designer who doesn't know the first thing about recruiting or hiring wrote the resume. That makes me question the content and how accurate it might be. It might sound good and be well-written, but is it real?

The advent of generative AI can assist with writing your resume, but it needs to be used correctly. For example, asking ChatGPT to write a resume for someone with your background might be tempting, but this isn't your best use of the technology. You'll end up with something generic that is full of buzzwords. While AI can help you write a resume, it must follow the format recommended in this chapter. This is what someone who reads hundreds of resumes a week wants to see.

AI can't invent your responsibilities or accomplishments without prompting.

Jeremy Schifeling wrote "The No. 1 AI Mistake Job Seekers Make, From a Career Expert: So Many People Use ChatGPT "in Exactly the Wrong Way'" and it is worth reading. Jeremy's recommendation is to start with a "draft resume written by a human (i.e., you). You need this to make the description of your experience your own. It's not something made up by a bot. Afterward, you can leverage ChatGPT to identify missing keywords and fine-tune your quantified accomplishments. Using generative AI will take some practice to master, but it can be highly useful."

ChatGPT can also help you fine-tune your professional summary, the description of your responsibilities and your accomplishments. ChatGPT can clarify, expound, and increase the overall impact of your resume. You also need to be sure it is in your voice and the descriptions are accurate. A resume written by ChatGPT may sound great, but is it really you?

There is no question generative AI can assist with your job search. If you haven't already, spend $59.99 to subscribe to the ChatGPT App, and see how it can help. I know there are other tools available, but that's the one I picked.

Key Messages

First and foremost, think about the reader and I don't mean an algorithm. You'll learn later how to apply without using the "Easy Apply" button. You need to keep it simple and follow a format like the one I outlined earlier. White space makes it easier for the reader to pick out your experience and accomplishments.

As backwards as it may sound, think about the responsibilities and accomplishments you want to share during your interview. As you flush out these thoughts, they become the content for your resume. It's all about results and outcomes so make sure the reader can clearly see how you made a difference.

The more you can customize your resume for any job you apply for, the better. If you think of the hiring manager as a consumer, they will only pull you off the shelf, if you look like a good fit.

Coaching Questions

- Will every reader know in the first sentence what you are and what makes you special?
- Have you made a clear distinction between responsibilities and results?
- How can you customer your resume so it speaks to reader

LinkedIn Is Just a Database

LinkedIn exists because it satisfies basic human needs—the need for attention, recognition, connection and affirmation. In truth, LinkedIn is perfectly designed to feed the narcissist in all of us. Ultimately, this is what allows LinkedIn to survive and thrive. We simply can't get enough of ourselves.

Why else would we endure an experience that seems to become more and more annoying?

The more we use LinkedIn, the more we expose ourselves to:

- A never-ending stream of solicitations
- Annoying posts about products and services we can't live without
- Advertisements
- Content we often don't care about

Here is the irony: anyone who uses LinkedIn regularly is a co-conspirator in their own misery. LinkedIn uses our own information to do what they do best: generate eyeballs and print money.

More recently, the content looks more and more like what you find on Facebook, which I dropped years ago. Although, I do like Facebook Marketplace because I can sell my junk, and then my junk belongs to someone else.

Because of the basic need LinkedIn satisfies and because it is so big, LinkedIn will be with us a long time. With all its frustrations,

Searching For A Job Sucks!

LinkedIn keeps us hooked. According to Mansoor Iqbal, LinkedIn made over $15.7 billion in annual revenue in 2023. For those of us who rely on LinkedIn for a living, we'll continue to pay the big bucks to use LinkedIn Recruiter.

If you have a free LinkedIn account, which is true for 69% of LinkedIn users, the LinkedIn experience is painful. For starters, the ability to search LinkedIn is terrible. You discover that as you learn about the other levels of LinkedIn that you can purchase. LinkedIn doesn't care about the free users, who are often job seekers. I certainly don't blame them for that, but let's call it what it is. For the free user, LinkedIn is an advertising platform.

And even if you pay, you encounter a product intentionally or unintentionally created for a challenging job search experience. You'd think a professional social network would make networking easier. However, other than helping you find people, you can't easily manage a networking campaign from LinkedIn. LinkedIn is the digital white pages, nothing more than a big-ass database that grows by the day because your absence would be conspicuous.

So, What Can You Do?

The ability to search any database is a function of how the data is collected and structured. The data collected by LinkedIn is user-generated and contains so much variability that searching LinkedIn is time-consuming and often difficult. As a recruiter, your ability to search a database becomes more important than your ability to recognize and evaluate talent.

For example, people choose their title when they sign up for LinkedIn. Searching by title is the most common way recruiters search LinkedIn. Yet, with all the variability in what people call themselves, it is a best-guess exercise, and many perfectly appropriate profiles get missed.

The best example of this is HR. Sometimes, the head of HR is a CHRO (Chief Human Resources Officer). Other times, they are the VP of HR, Chief People Officer, Chief of Talent or Culture, Chief Human Capital Officer, or Chief People & Change Management Officer. When you choose titles that are less common, you become more challenging to find. Keep it simple and use a title that most people recognize.

The use of keywords is also important when writing your LinkedIn Profile. Using keywords is the other way recruiters search. One way to determine keywords is to review job descriptions for the same role and identify the ones you see repeated. Those are the keywords that probably matter most. Another more automated way is to use the Job Description Keyword Finder on Tealhq.com. This is a more analytical approach and will provide some deeper insight.

After using LinkedIn for many years, I am convinced people don't understand the difference between what they do functionally versus their industry. For example, an HR person working in Telecomm will indicate their industry as HR versus Telecomm. Really?

I always wonder what company the Company Size Filter option is selecting. Is it my current organization or one 10 years ago?

Searching For A Job Sucks!

I must say I find it unusual when someone doesn't have a profile picture. As a recruiter, the absence of a photo is code that someone isn't going to be interested, so don't waste your time. If you have a profile picture and want to see how good it is, test out Snapper Photo Analyzer. It's free and provides useful, actionable feedback.

Your LinkedIn profile is a searchable page, so keywords matter. It is easier to search when more information is on your LinkedIn profile. The amount of information you provide seriously influences the ability to get found.

Ideally, your LinkedIn profile is a smaller version of your resume with a clear statement of responsibilities for each job and a bullet list of accomplishments.

In my experience, recruiters using LinkedIn Recruiter, use job titles, locations, industries, and locations to find the most relevant matches. The LinkedIn profiles with the most matches appear at the top of the page.

I am often asked whether you need to respond each time a recruiter reaches out to you. The answer is an emphatic "yes!" Even if you aren't interested now, these are important connections you'll want to maintain for as long as you can. In terms of how to reply, aijobs.ai published an article, "How to Respond to a Recruiter on Linked," which provides good advice.

The only addition to these messages that I strongly suggest is an offer to help. For example, "I would be happy to introduce you to anyone in my network if you would find that helpful. I'll also recommend anyone I think would be a good fit." You want recruiters to see you as a helpful resource and ally. This way, when you need their assistance, you increase the likelihood they will get back to you.

There has been lots of discussion about the "Open to Work" feature on LinkedIn. To some recruiters, it signals you are unemployed and/or desperate. That means you are less desirable as a candidate. It's like you are standing on the corner wearing a sandwich board asking for work. When I'm recruiting and have an open position to fill and you are exactly the person I'm looking for, I will reach out to you even if you don't have that feature turned on, so why raise the question? To me, there is no advantage to putting that designation on your LinkedIn profile so why bother?

In fact, I often tell people to not change their status if they are no longer with their current company. Again, it's just another indication that something might be wrong. Just tell the recruiter you haven't gotten around to changing your profile. Hopefully, by the time the question gets asked, you've sold yourself as the ideal candidate.

In a December 9, 2022, article for Medium, Katie Jacquez offers the following four tips to attract more recruiters

First, she recommends using the Name and Headline to say more and provide more context about who you are. The example she uses is "Harrison Wheeler, design manager at LinkedIn and the host of the Technically Speaking podcast."

I'm not a huge fan of lots of content where the title belongs. As a recruiter, I focus on titles; all the other words are just a distraction

Searching For A Job Sucks!

when I am trying to find people. I can read all the other stuff in your description.

Katie says the About section is where you tell your story. This can be an overview of your professional experience and journey—but keep it short. No one likes to read. If this is just a rehash of what you have under Experience section, it's kind of a waste. Add something here that provides more context for your search. For example, why are your skills in one functional area easily transferable to another. You can also include contact information, so you are easy to reach.

After I find you, the Experience section is what matters most. Many people mess up their profiles by not distinguishing between responsibilities and accomplishments. You can tailor this information for the kind of role you are seeking. Be sure to indicate each job at the same company as it shows career growth and progress.

Katie's advice for the Skills section is to reorder your list of skills so the top three skills align with your job search. Remember that whoever has the most skills doesn't win. Remove those skills that aren't relevant to your current job search. The Skills section matters most for non-executive-level jobs. I have to admit I don't know if I have ever paid attention to the Skills section. I am far more interested in where you work, what you are, your responsibilities, and accomplishments. A review and assessment of your actual skills comes later.

As much as it pains me to say, if you are a serious, active job seeker, buying a paid version of LinkedIn might be worthwhile to support your search. LinkedIn Premium makes it easier to connect with recruiters and hiring managers. You get additional capabilities like InMail messages to out-of-network individuals, comparative applicant data, insight into your profile views, and advanced search filters. Ultimately, LinkedIn Premium allows you to expand your network beyond your immediate connections. Rachael Gilpin wrote the article "Is LinkedIn Premium Worth It? An In-Depth Guide for Job Seekers." After reading Rachael's article, you can decide for yourself, but I recommend investing to turbocharge your job search.

Once you land your job, cancel your paid subscription and get to work. In my experience, the people using LinkedIn are job seekers, people promoting themselves or people trying to sell something. The people I know who are busy and working hard spend very little, if any, time on LinkedIn.

On the other hand, if you want to hear from people you don't know and learn about their child's graduation from college or pictures from someone's vacation read on! Just remember to look up periodically —you never know what you might be missing in the real world.

Key Messages

If you are job seeker, your goal is to get found. For that reason, you need a profile that will attract recruiters. It is important to make a clear distinction between responsibilities and accomplishment like you do on your resume. The more you can quantify your accomplishments the better.

If you are a job seeker, paying for a Premium version of LinkedIn will be a good investment. Once you land, downgrade to a free version and get to work.

Searching For A Job Sucks!

Coaching Questions

- How can your LinkedIn profile better serve your job search?

- Do you know the titles and keywords recruiters use to search?

- Once you land, how can you continue to network with your most important connections outside of LinkedIn?

Lessons from Job Seekers

Finding a Job is a Job

Jerry is a 54-year-old sales leader with 32 years of sales management experience who excels at leading sales teams and in the technology space and growing businesses. He is currently a Regional President for his current organization.

Jerry wasn't looking for a job, but with a new Chief Executive Officer (CEO) and other changes at his previous company, Jerry had questions about what he saw happening. While he wasn't actively looking, if something came across his Gmail, he would open the email and read it.

Jerry's current role came about when the Chief Operating Officer (COO) reached out to him with an opportunity. The COO is a former colleague from two companies ago and they have stayed close making a point to talk every four or five months. The conversations were mostly about family and vacations until he hit Jerry with a "What if?" That turned into a lot more conversations and a meeting with the CEO, and he was hooked.

Jerry was only looking for about three or four months before he landed his current role. Jerry believes strongly that until you make finding a full-time job your full-time job, you're not going to find it.

Throwing your name at a few postings leads to failure. If you are looking for a senior level role you need to treat it like a high-level prospect.

Searching For A Job Sucks!

The key is finding out who the hiring manager is and go directly to them. Go around HR, go around everyone and send them a direct correspondence. If a smart executive sees your background and believes you can solve their problem, they will have someone reach out to you. No one likes filling jobs and if they see a way to get it done, they will be interested.

Reflecting on his search, Jerry made the point that no one is a professional job seeker. The average person doesn't even know where to begin. Do I update my resume? If so, what is the best way to do it. What most people want is someone to hold their hand and spoon-feed them through the process. This is especially true for someone who is gainfully employed with a full-time job that occupies 50-plus hours a week. If they have a family, they don't have the time to invest in a job search. Jerry believes people are either doing it wrong or not dedicating the number of hours necessary to be successful, so they need somebody that can do a lot or the work for them.

You can reach out to lots of executive recruiters, but you rarely hear a helpful response. Jerry would be willing to pay a fee-based engagement of $5K or $10K to find the right new opportunity. There are firms out there that provide that service. The problem with those arrangements is that there has to be the right job available to make that work. If your timing is off, that job may not exist. There is also so much these services can't control: like your ability to interview well that makes the investment risky. Some of these firms share your picture and resume with hundreds of search firms. I often wonder how that is perceived.

CHAPTER 1: PREPARE - No One Cares Who You Are If You Can't Be Clear about What You Are

It was frustrating for Jerry to be in front of so many opportunities and the length of time different opportunities would take to close. He would have multiple interviews for one job and three to four months would pass with no answer. He understands that things change. In one case, the job was eliminated after multiple interviews because of restructuring. In another case, the Senior Vice President (SVP) hiring manager was ousted.

In Jerry's experience, it is hard to break out when you have been in one industry your entire career—medical devices, copiers, telecom, and so on. You get pigeonholed, which is very difficult. This is why your network is so important. Your relationships can help you break out from long-held stereotypes. Staying in touch with those very close connections is critical to the long-term success of your career.

As he matures in his career, Jerry needs to be convinced that a new opportunity is the right one for him. Don't go just for a job. Understand the environment, understand the culture, and hear that from multiple levels of the organization. You hear from the C-suite making $15M a year that the culture is amazing and a middle manager who says the place is a grind every day, there is terrible turnover, and the culture is awful, but it's all sunshine and lollipops at the top of the organization.

If he had it to do over, he would have been more prepared for how long it would take. It's not arrogance, just being misinformed and a little naïve.

Jerry's advice is to start looking before you need to look and to keep in touch with your network. Most people aren't professional job seekers, and you need someone who can help you navigate the process.

Everyone Can Be an A Player If They Are in the Right Role

Max is a 59-year-old sales executive with a successful track record selling enterprise digital solutions to large companies. He has worked in the same industry 30 years and is a highly recognized leader. His role is to develop market strategies and drive revenue, which means he needs to build teams by putting people in the right roles to succeed.

Max believes we all have strengths and he learned that lesson early in his career. Those strengths fit somewhere, so it's important to know what you are good at. To learn this, you can take assessments or have people tell you, but it's important to go down a path that plays to your strengths. In his view, this is how you have a successful career.

Figuring out where you fit is very important. This can start as early as high school and continue right into college and beyond. If you speak to 10 people, 9 will tell you they are doing something different than what they studied in school. That's why you need to be open to: the art of the possible based on your skills and strengths that can likely fit in many places. The earlier you understand that in your career, the better.

Max went to school to be a teacher and coach because he played sports. When he combined his passion with his financial objectives, he found himself as a sales leader, which was very similar to leading a sports team. He has transferred his leadership capability to a

CHAPTER 1: PREPARE - No One Cares Who You Are If You Can't Be Clear about What You Are

different environment. He has done different roles with different companies, but he has applied the same transferable skills.

Max started looking for a new opportunity when he realized the company he was working for wasn't what they had advertised. He had been hired to start a new SaaS-based digital business inside an older firm that wanted to transform itself. Max loves to build scale and grow businesses. This role fit his style and desire to embrace ambiguity, take risks, and learn. Eventually, he learned this 50-year-old company wasn't ready to move in a digital direction and didn't invest in the platform to make that happen. He realized it wasn't the cultural fit he wanted long term.

An executive recruiter reached out to Max, which is how he landed in his current role. Max believes searching for a job is a full-time endeavor. He tells people if they are committed to making a move, they need a plan and they need to leverage their network. You need to build a network throughout your career, and you need to give back to that network, not just take. Max learned to invest in his network—advice, introductions, and so on.

Max talked a lot about having a plan. What do you want to do, what target companies offer those roles, and who in your network is connected to those companies. He believes you need to treat your job search like a project. It starts with having a target. You want to be in XYZ role by a certain date. Then work backward—what do you need to do today, this week, next week, and the next month? For example, you need to network with 10 people this week. The real power is to connect with hiring managers. The goal is to have someone refer you into the right person. Short of that, you reach out directly via

Searching For A Job Sucks!

LinkedIn or email. Max uses his network to make the right introductions.

People will often under-value what they have accomplished and the transferable skills they possess. With greater self-awareness, it is possible to pursue opportunities you might not think are possible. This means you need to be open to other perspectives from other people. People who are more experienced can point out ways and fields where your skills can be applied that you haven't even considered. Building professional relationships early on is the key to gaining this insight that can change your career. Max had someone early in his career who recognized his potential even though he didn't have experience in sales, but he saw the raw skills, the willingness to take risks, and made the introductions that launched a highly successful career. Max now takes the time to give back to other professionals. Start your network early so you get words of wisdom that you can't learn in school.

It took him about six months to land a new role when he decided it was time to look for the new opportunity. What he found most challenging is that you have to kiss a lot of frogs. You see a lot of roles, but you often need to learn more to really understand the requirements and responsibilities. Max's advice is get enough information about the role before making a decision.

Max always takes the call when a recruiter calls in hopes of building a relationship and passing along people who might be a fit so he can be helpful.

What he found frustrating was interviewing with someone who wasn't prepared. You can tell when someone is asking general

CHAPTER 1: PREPARE -No One Cares Who You Are If You Can't Be Clear about What You Are

questions and quickly asks what questions you have. Most hiring managers are under-prepared, so you need to be over-prepared. What do you want someone to know about you before the end of the interview?

As a hiring manager himself, he finds HR people frustrating because they can't always see beyond the perfect profile that checks every box. They will often miss what other capabilities a candidate might possess and how else they might fit. He finds it disappointing when people can't see outside the lines.

It is also disappointing as a candidate to not receive feedback after an interview. You can't learn from the experience when you don't know what went wrong. He still recommends that you ask, but have low expectations.

Max often refers to the importance of having a plan. You want each move in your career to be thoughtful and to move you along your plan. You want to apply the feedback you receive to make mid-course corrections that get you more on track.

Max also believes it is important to have references from different levels. This is how you validate your candidacy. People will do their own references so you want to nurture your network so they respond positively when someone reaches out to them.

In the last three years, more interviews are not face-to-face but over Zoom. Max's learning and advice is practice and get feedback on how you come across.

Max believes the key to success is knowing your brand—what you are good at. That is the headline that will grab attention? Who you are and what you are good at stated clearly and succinctly. Know your strengths and how you add value. This helps you evaluate opportunities that come your way and determine if they are a good fit.

Max also wanted to make the point that as a candidate—you have choice. While you are interviewing you also need to determine if this is the right culture, the right opportunity. Fill your pipeline so you can decide so you have options. Most of all, it is okay to say "no." If you say

"yes" to something that is wrong, in six months you'll be looking again. It is better to say "no," than be told "no." The fit has to work for everyone.

Look in the Mirror

Rhonda is a 61-year-old Chief People Officer for a start-up. Prior to that, she has led HR for several large companies. She has worked in human resources for 40 years, and describes herself as a dot connector and problem solver who can find creative solutions for organizations to help them grow.

Rhonda wasn't looking when she was contacted by someone who knew the CEO of her current company. Rhonda went on to say that she doesn't consider herself a strong networker, but she has almost never had to look for a job. She prefers to build relationships as opposed to feeling like she is networking. People have contacted her about new opportunities her entire career. When someone says they are out building their network, it seems inauthentic to make connections you are only using to find a job. She has frequently been contacted by former colleagues with whom she had a strong relationship.

Culture, values, and the leaders are important to her when considering new opportunities. If you can find the right combination of those three while doing work you love, that is the ideal.

What she found most challenging was leaving a strong team and flicking the off switch the day she left the office for the last time. She no longer had the social connection or the personal validation she got every day at work. It's like she lost her purpose and felt a bit lost.

Culture matters, and it is hard for a job seeker to figure it out. Rhonda's previous company had a culture that was more missionary when she joined and turned more mercenary as they grew. Early on, people cared for one another and that radically shifted to a greater focus on growth and bringing in lots of leaders who don't share the same values. She has seen culture become optics. They are just words on a paper.

She would tell a job seeker to find someone in the business they know or someone who might know someone in the business to get an accurate picture of the culture. You can look on Glassdoor or Indeed, but the people who comment on those sites are the ones that didn't have a good experience, so you won't' get a balanced picture of the culture. It is more about venting and blowing off steam. Find someone in your network who can give you the inside scoop on an organization.

Searching For A Job Sucks!

Rhonda was overwhelmed by the amount of outreach and felt obligated to respond. You need to think of your job search as a full-time effort. Don't come across as desperate. You could say, "I've been out of work, please consider me," but that isn't how you get a job. You need to leverage your network, and most people don't put enough time and effort into nurturing their most important relationships. If you are out of a job, go to events and see who you are connected to on LinkedIn. She also sees lots of headhunters who might be worth contacting.

Don't wait to start networking until you need to find a job. The relationships you build beforehand will eventually pay off.

Rhonda's strongest advice is to think about why you may not have succeeded in your last role. If you were let go, you need to ask yourself why and own your contribution to the outcome. If you were part of a mass layoff, why were you chosen? You need to ask yourself how you found yourself on the list. Is there a skill gap? Do you need to set more realistic objectives for the next job? For the most part, companies don't let go of their strongest performers. It is time to do some soul searching and ask yourself how you contributed to being let go. You need to take accountability for something that was off. What prevents you from bringing your best self to the job? Is there a disconnect in regards to values that you recognize that makes it hard for you to be yourself and do your best? Take some time to figure out what you need to differently in the future.

Her other advice is never jump too quickly. Do the research to know what you are getting into. Sometimes you need to take a step down to find something fun you will enjoy and do well. You need to go after what is realistic. We all have limits.

CHAPTER 2: SEARCH

The Job Board Abyss

Let's start with a question: How often have you applied for a job on a job board and all you hear is—crickets. And then you wonder, what happened? Did someone see my resume? Did someone review my background and experience? Why isn't anyone calling? Should I send it again? Is it time to order pizza and stream "Stranger Things" for the third time??

Applying for a job online is a double-edged sword. On the one hand, it can be very easy. For example, LinkedIn has its Easy Apply button. While sitting on your couch, with one eye on LinkedIn and the other on *The Bachelor* or *Sports Center*, you can apply for 30 jobs in about 10 minutes. It doesn't get much easier than that. The danger here is you think you have actually done something productive.

At the same time, resumes flood into applicant tracking systems (ATSs) that manage and track applications. Using keywords, recruiters can set specific parameters for automated resume screening. You won't get reviewed if you don't have the right keywords. You are also hearing more about artificial intelligence (AI) and machine learning (ML) that can help recruiters automate the screening process using various forms of analysis. The candidate with the most keywords as opposed to someone who might be the best candidate, get seen.

So, while it is super easy to apply on a job board, the result is a terrible consumer experience that job seekers complain about endlessly. I don't mean to sound harsh when I say this, but truthfully, no one cares. I know human resources (HR) and recruiters love to wax on about the candidate experience and how much it matters to the hiring process. Unfortunately, at least while employers have the upper hand, it's all just talk. Looking at where employers spend their time and money, you can see it's all about creating efficiency. The technology is more about screening you out versus screening you in.

To understand the importance of job boards, you need to know how an internal recruiter spends their time. Recruiters perform 3 main tasks: research, sourcing, and recruiting

Research and sourcing are what recruiters do when they are actively looking for and reaching out to candidates to get their attention. Research and sourcing are very time-consuming and resource intensive.

Recruiting is what recruiters do when they get a candidate's attention and work to engage them in the hiring process. These three terms often get used interchangeably, but they are very different. The reason this distinction matters to job seekers is because companies often under invest in research and sourcing. Hence, recruiters rely heavily on job boards to generate applicant flow.

As the head of staffing, I was shocked by how little time and effort our recruiters spent researching and searching for candidates. Aside from the 3 main tasks, recruiters spend lots of time entering data into an ATS, generating reports for status meetings with their boss and senior leadership, attending intake meetings with hiring managers, participating in staff meetings to discuss why open positions remain open, handling referrals, and processing paperwork.

The bottom line is recruiters rely heavily on job boards to generate applicant flow. That is why job boards remain relevant and will be with us for a long time.

There is another reality associated with job boards, which has to do with the posted content. Job postings are typically nothing more than HR job descriptions posted online. Those documents may have been created weeks, months, or years ago. They don't always reflect the requirements to fill a role—today! It is unlikely they reflect the problem the hiring manager is trying to solve. You often see lots of "soft" stuff around culture and interpersonal skills; remember, HR writes these documents to scope a job, pay a job, and to be in compliance with the latest regulations. The hardcore technical or functional skills required to solve problems or tackle opportunities are absent. When the requirements are wrong, how can you expect a response when replying to a job posted online?

There is another fatal flaw in the process, which happens at the beginning of the recruiting process. When a recruiter starts a search, they often meet with the hiring manager and ask questions about the open position to understand the requirements. Unfortunately, hiring managers are not always prepared for those conversations. What a recruiter hears is what the manager can think of at that moment without lots of thought. There is nothing analytical about those conversations; they represent one person's perspective, and the hiring

Searching For A Job Sucks!

manager is often in a hurry to get to their next meeting. Recruiters leave those meetings with a laundry list of requirements and do not understand what matters most. As someone on the receiving end of these meetings, I have been shocked by how often managers can't articulate what they need. It isn't unusual for a manager to use the recruiting process to figure it out as they begin to see candidates. This is another reason why the "content" on a job board doesn't reflect the job's requirements and why you may not hear back when you apply for a job online.

The other reality associated with the quality of content on a job board is whether the job is genuinely open. Job boards love lots of content, so it is in their best interest to leave postings online as long as possible—even after a job has been closed. You won't know that and will still wonder why no one has replied. You will wonder even more after the same job reappears after being removed sometime earlier.

A 2023 article by Brennan Zagami for CompXL reported that as many as one-third of the job postings are fake. This means that one-third of your time looking at jobs online may be a waste. A company may post a job to give the impression an organization is growing and needs to hire. Sometimes, an organization will post to gather resumes for future openings. So, many jobs you are anxiously waiting to hear about do not even exist.

And finally, you won't be surprised to learn that recruiting firms sometimes post jobs simply to gather resumes. You can tell when the description does not mention a hiring organization and sounds generic.

The firm may specialize in a particular discipline and use this tactic to gather resumes and get a leg up on its recruiting firm competitors. If a recruiting firm can grow its database of resumes, it can respond to a client's request faster and earn a fee. Don't kid yourself; the fee, not the customer experience, matters here.

Do job boards serve a purpose, and can you find a job via a job board? The answer is "yes." However, you need to calibrate your expectations. It's unlikely you will ever hear from someone and don't count on a job board to find your next job. If it works, great! But otherwise, stop being disappointed.

So, What Can You Do?

The alternative I offer may sound radical, but it will get you more attention.

Stop applying online for jobs you see posted on job boards.

If a job board represents the front door, you must start sneaking in the back door. How? I recommend you go directly to the hiring manager or a recruiter.

The first step is to identify the company that has the open position. Often, the name of the organization is on the posting. If a search firm posts the job, you can also see the firm's name. There will also be cases where the name of the person receiving resumes is in the body of the posting. With some detective work, this isn't too difficult to figure out.

Once you know the organization's name, LinkedIn can be a big help. You'll want to search by the company's name and the department

Searching For A Job Sucks!

hiring to find a hiring manager. For example, if you are using a free version of LinkedIn, put the name of the company AND human resources, or marketing or information technology, and so on in the search bar and hit enter. For example: "Hewlett Packard" AND "Human Resources." The result will be a list of people you can scroll through to find someone who might be the right contact.

If you have a paid version of LinkedIn, searching is much easier. A paid version of LinkedIn is a good investment if you are looking for a job.

Once you figure out, to the best of your ability, who the hiring manager might be, you need to craft a short, eye-catching email that will hopefully get their attention. You are hoping for one of three outcomes:

- The receiver forwards the email to HR and asks them to contact you.

- The receiver sends your email to the recruiter responsible for filling the role, internal or external, and asks them to contact you.

- The receiver sends you a note back or asks their assistant to reach out to set up a call.

While this may seem bold, what have you got to lose? If you go through the job posting system, you will get lost in an ATS.

You need to understand that when a manager has an open position to fill, it's because they have a problem to solve or see an opportunity to tackle. The manager feels pain and needs to quickly get the right person in this role. A job opening takes them away from what they must accomplish daily. For a manager, having to hire someone means they get to work twice as hard. In addition to their day job, they have to meet with a recruiter to determine hiring requirements, review resumes, get team members ready to interview, screen candidates, and hire someone. If you've ever done that, you know it isn't fun or easy. It's a huge distraction. If your resume appears at the top of the pile and seems like the perfect solution, it will get attention. The key is getting to the top of the pile, and this is the best way to make that happen.

The following **sample email** can used as a template for going direct.

Subject: COO opportunity at Joe's Bowling and Billiards

Dear Ms. Smith,

I am writing to apply for your COO opportunity at (name of company).

My background as a COO includes a long track record of success in large and small companies, maximizing operational and financial efficiency.

Examples of my accomplishments include:

- *Launched personnel realignment, accounting, and technology initiatives for the General Accounting and Project Accounting teams of a $500M+ real estate development group, resulting in decreased cycle time and increased reporting accuracy.*

Searching For A Job Sucks!

- *Managed a team of 15 CPAs to efficiently analyze and restate three years of public financial information for a $1+B nonprofit public benefit corporation, helping it avoid a significant financial default. Reported to the Board of Directors.*

- *Optimized operations for a real estate developer with a $250+M portfolio by restructuring the technology infrastructure and providing management with greater access to operating and financial information.*

I would like to learn more about the challenges facing (name of company) and discuss how I can contribute to your success. I look forward to speaking at your convenience.

Sincerely,

Jeffrey

Let's unpack what makes an email introduction like this work.

1. It is short. People are busy and don't have time to read. If someone sees too many words, they may check out.

2. The purpose is concise and clear.

3. There is a short statement that immediately speaks to qualifications.

4. There are eye-catching, easy-to-read bullets highlighting accomplishments that speak directly to the requirements.

5. There is a short closing with a clear call to action.

You don't see many words and fluff around stuff anyone can say about themselves. At this point in the process, I don't care if you are a good team player with strong interpersonal skills with great integrity. If those soft skills matter, that will come out in the process. I only care if you can solve my problem or opportunity.

Here is another example from **someone with less professional experience**:

Subject: Deputy Field Director Opportunity

Dear Bernie,

I am writing to apply for the Deputy Field Director, Member Mobilization position for the League of Conservation Voters.

My previous experience working on multiple campaigns and my leadership skills make me an exceptionally qualified candidate for this position. I am very excited to learn more about this opportunity.

The following skills and previous work experience make me an excellent candidate for the role.

I have worked on six state and federal campaigns and know how to plan and execute a

campaign program.

- *I can mobilize and work on multiple projects at once.*
- *I have experience developing and coordinating field training.*

Searching For A Job Sucks!

• *I effectively build coalitions and keep key players current on critical projects.*

My attached resume demonstrates my passion for campaigns and politics.

I look forward to speaking with you in greater depth about my background and experience and how I can be a valuable member of your staff.

Kindest regards,

Donnie

Here is a similar example for **someone graduating from college and applying for their first job.**

Subject: Internship Opportunity

Dear Hiring Team,

I am writing to apply for a position with the Green Corps Field School for Environmental Organizing for 2023–2024. I am a senior at the University of Vermont majoring in public communications and minoring in political science and community international development.

My current classes focus on public policy, sustainability, community development, public administration, and social marketing.

I am attracted to a position with Green Corps for the following reasons:

- *I am committed to serving communities, as demonstrated by my community service work in Belize.*

- *I am committed to sustainability, as evidenced by my Green America work.*

- *I worked at Smart Growth Vermont to support towns and counties in planning and developing sustainable communities.*

- *I am extremely task-oriented and can handle many projects simultaneously.*

- *I am a team player who will work well with staff and community members.*

My attached resume will show that I am active on campus and contribute to the University community. I will bring this same energy, enthusiasm, and commitment to a position with Green Corps.

I look forward to speaking with you in greater depth about my background and the contribution I can make to your organization. You may contact me with any questions at (insert email and phone number). Thank you for your time and consideration.

Sincerely,

Margaret Thatcher

The format for all three examples is the same regardless of your years of experience. The outline can be used anytime you want to apply directly. Expressing confidence and capability is essential as well as focusing on what you have accomplished and what you can contribute.

The strategy I am recommending more and more is to send a much shorter, email and embed your resume in the email. Your objective isn't to get a callback. Your objective is to be seen, and this is a way to make that happen. Here is an example:

Subject: CMO Opportunity

Hi Michael,

My name is Andy Bernard and I am an accomplished CMO with experience at Paychex, CDW, and HubSpot.

I see you are hiring for a Head of Marketing. I am very interested in learning more about the opportunity. My resume is below.

Please let me know when you have time to set up an introductory conversation.

Thank you so much,

Andy Bernard

I like this approach because the email is short. It can be scanned quickly, and the first line is where you articulate your value proposition based on what you think will get the readers attention. In this case, it's brand names the recipient will recognize. In other cases, it might be technologies you know and use, an accomplishment the reader will find interesting, a problem you have solved, or a referral from somebody. It's whatever hook you can use to get their attention.

Putting the resume in the body of the resume is hard to miss. If you are the right person and can solve the hiring mangers problem, you will hear back. If not, you won't so what do you have to lose?

Going direct takes more time, so I would focus on jobs where you see a perfect fit. Not where you think you are close, or where you think you could do the job, or where you are just attracted to the title. I understand this is subjective, but when you are honest with yourself, you'll stop wasting precious time.

This strategy depends on your ability to email someone directly. If you are wondering how to find someone's email it isn't that difficult. There are some standard email structures; if you know those, you can use an email tester like hunter.io to know if you have it right. You can also send an email and see if it bounces.

Start by trying these six:

1. firstname.lastname@website.com

2. firstname@website.com

3. firstinitiallastname@website.com

4. firstname_lastname@website.com

5. lastnamefirstinitial@website.com

6. firstnamelastinitial@website.com

Another resource is Raghav Tayal's article "9 Ways to Find Anyone's Email Address in 2024 (Tried and Tested)." Raghav included a comprehensive list of email testers that you can use to figure out someone's work email.

There is another recruiter trick you may find helpful. You can try *@companydomain.com. *@ is a wildcard in Boolean search and will bring up everything that ends in nameofcompany.com. It might be cumbersome, but as you scroll through the results, you may eventually see someone who works at the company with the exact email structure you need to go directly to them

There is a way you can test emails to see if they are correct. Hunter.io gives you 25 free email verifications a month.

People have asked me many times what to do if they don't get a response. My advice is to wait five business days and try again. Using the previous example, you can change the subject to *Joe's Bowling and Billiards COO Opportunity*. You can then send the same email. If they saw it the first time and ignored it, so what? They can ignore it again.

On the other hand, if they missed it the first time, they now have all the relevant information. This strategy will likely take some persistence. Be respectful and don't assume the worst. If you don't hear back after the second time, it's time to either find another person to contact or move on to another opportunity.

The other way to jump the line is to find someone to make an internal referral. I get asked regularly if I know someone and if I can make a warm introduction. If you have an existing relationship, most people are happy to help. The place to find these possible referral sources is LinkedIn. If you have many connections in a particular organization, it might be cumbersome, but if you see someone, getting a warm introduction puts you in a great place to get attention.

Subject: Hi from Tom Smith

Hi Jerry,

I hope this finds you well and keeping busy.

I'm reaching out to ask a favor. There is a job at ADP posted on LinkedIn. I want to apply for Job #238751, Director of Sales Operations. The title and description fit perfectly with my background, and I'm interested in learning more.

Do you know who this job might report to? If not, I certainly understand ADP is a huge organization. Could you send my resume directly to the hiring manager? I'm trying to get ahead of all the resumes submitted via the online posting. If you can get an employee referral bonus, even better.

I appreciate any assistance you can provide. Let's catch up soon when you have some time.

Thanks so much,

Tom

The other angle to take here is to find people you know who used to work for the organization. While they may be gone, they may still know the hiring manager and be willing to make an introduction.

Subject: Hi from Tom Smith

Searching For A Job Sucks!

Hi Jerry,

I hope this finds you well and keeping busy.

I'm reaching out to ask a favor. While I know you no longer work at ADP, a job at ADP posted on LinkedIn has caught my attention. I want to apply for Job #238751, Director of Sales Operations. The title and description fit perfectly with my background, and I'm interested in learning more.

Do you know the hiring manager? Or do you know someone on the team? If not, I understand that ADP is a huge organization, and you've been gone for a while. Would you mind sending my resume directly to the hiring manager if you do? I'm trying to get ahead of all the resumes via the online posting.

I appreciate any assistance you can provide. Let's catch up soon when you have some time.

Thanks so much,

Tom

If you can't leverage a personal connection, the third option is to take your best guess about who might be the hiring manager or manager in the chain of command and reach out to them directly.

Subject: Director of Sales Operations Posting

Hi Jerry,

My name is Liza Smith, and I am very interested in the Director of Sales Operations role at ADP.

I spent the last five years as a Sales Operations Manager at Paychex. I was able to accomplish the following:

- *Optimized our sales processes, and we grew sales by 15% year over year.*

- *Conducted research and analyzed data to create accurate sales forecasts, contributing to our sales planning process.*

- *Trained over 150 salespeople each year.*

The title and description fit my background perfectly, and I'm interested in learning more.

I would appreciate the opportunity for an introductory call.

Thank you for your time,

Liza

These emails can be modified to sound like you and to address the specific opportunity. The message is simple: go direct. Don't play by the rules. Be the resume on a manager's desk that perfectly solves their problem. If that is truly you, you may hear from someone very quickly.

The other question that often gets asked is how to find the names of hiring managers. While this may not be a perfect science, there are ways to figure it out using LinkedIn.

Search by organization and look for people with the same job title. From here you can see people in this role and who they are connected to. It's not uncommon for someone to be connected to their boss. Often times, the pop up on the right side of the screen will show connections. Are any of them managers or directors? Click show more to see what else you can find. Even if it isn't the correct Manager or Director, they may know who is and when you reach out, if they like what they see, will forward your resume.

Another way is to search by Director or Manager title in the function and you might see someone that looks like the right person. If you click show more, it will give you more options to choose from. Once you find someone who looks correct, use the email hacks to find the best email.

If the response back is to apply online, then you have done your best. You may not hear back but at least you've been seen.

Sometimes you might find the name of the recruiter in the posting. Even when you do, my first recommendation is to find the hiring manager or someone else in the hierarchy where this role reports. I would avoid VP or C-suite individuals unless that's who the role reports to.

Key Messages

Stop applying for jobs online. You can't trust the job posting system to work in your favor. Go direct to someone who might be the hiring manager or the recruiter. If you don't know for sure who that is, get as close as you can and take your best shot. Keep your message short and copy and paste your resume in the email. The goal is to be seen and to not get lost in a database.

This strategy works when you only apply for jobs that are close to an exact match. There is a big difference between your interest in a job or desire to do a job and your actual qualifications. You may believe you can do the job but the person who posted that job is looking for an exact fit.

Going direct doesn't mean you will hear something back. It does, however, increase your odds of being seen. If you are truly a good fit and can solve someone's problem, you significantly increase your odds of success.

Coaching Questions

- What worries you about going direct?

- What do you have to lose?

- Who can you contact the next time you see a job posted online that you find interesting?

Searching For A Job Sucks!

You Don't Pick a Search Firm; They Pick You

What can you realistically expect from search firms and recruiters? The answer for most people is a probably not much. I hate being so harsh, but I'm afraid that's true. John Sumser reported in a *HR Examiner* article titled "The Odds of Getting a Job with a Recruiter," that "Fewer than seven percent of the workforce is <u>ever</u> contacted by a recruiter." He said, "The odds are 1 in 12 (8.5%) that a recruiter will ever call you." Even worse, "...the overall odds are about 1 in 28,520 (.0035%) that your conversation with a headhunter will land you a job." As you can see from the math, unless you are one of the very best at what you do, and even if you are, the odds of being placed by a search firm are minuscule.

Does this mean you abandon search firms or headhunters as part of your job search? No, but you must understand how search firms operate to improve your success rate.

For starters, a search firm makes money only if it develops a reputation for presenting excellent talent and for making placements. For this reason, search consultants have limited time and can only pay attention to candidates with immediate value. You may want and even expect someone to call you back after sending a search firm your resume, but they simply don't have the capacity. Search firms are under the same time and cost restraints as everyone else.

Here is the other challenge. Search firms fill a small percentage of available openings at any given time. What are the odds that a recruiter is working on an assignment that matches your background at the exact time you call? Slim at best.

Furthermore, search firms prefer to work with people they know and trust, and they rely heavily on their network. Unsolicited resumes might get attention, but they need to stand out.

Search firms are highly biased toward people in the market versus on the market. Connecting with a search firm when you are unemployed is more difficult. They have a strong bias that the best people are still working.

So, What Can You Do?

Here are some important points to remember when working with search firms.

- Be ready when they call. Know what you are and what you want to do. It's not a search firm's responsibility to figure this out for you; they are not career counselors. Have this well rehearsed so it is clear and concise.

- Have an updated resume that speaks to your responsibilities and accomplishments. Get rid of the fluff and the long lists of self-professed competencies. No one cares, and without context, they are meaningless.

- If you are lucky and get called by a search firm, you must understand and respect their process. Remember, they are not working for you. They are working for the client that pays them. They will stay engaged as long as it makes sense—not a second longer.

- A search consultant will talk with many people to find the right fit for their client. If that isn't you, you may not hear back from them. I know that seems rude, but that's the reality. You can be sure the opportunity has passed after you've followed up a couple of times and haven't heard anything back.

- It's okay to follow up with a search firm periodically—once every three to six months is usually enough, and email is preferred. More often than that, you begin to look desperate.

The best way to endear yourself to the search consultant is to be useful long before you need or are ready to look for a job. Provide them with industry trends, insights about possible candidates, or helpful news about specific companies. Offering and being of assistance increases the chance of building a relationship that someday may pay dividends.

Be aware that search firms have a bias against people who are unemployed. That is the other reason why building a relationship in advance is so critical. If they don't know you and you are unemployed, good luck.

Not all recruiters are the same. Some recruiters specialize by industry and or discipline. Recruit has a directory of executive search firms, recruiters, or headhunters that you may find helpful and is located at https://www.i-recruit.com/recruiters-directory.php. Find the right person at the firm and reach out to them directly. *Forbes* also publishes a list each year of the top executive search firms. The 2024 listing is at https://shorturl.at/oHeH8.

CHAPTER 2: SEARCH - The Job Board Abyss

If you are looking for nonprofit executive-level opportunities, you might find this directory helpful: https://www.i-recruit.com/speciality/nonprofit-recruiters.

Another resource you might find helpful is the member directory for the Association of Executive Search and Leadership Consultants (AESC). https://www.aesc.org/search-firms

Scroll through the list and find firms that align with your background and interests.

Outside of the directories just mentioned, Chaymae Samir wrote an article for Zety titled "How to Find a Headhunter or Recruiter to Get You a Job Now." She provided helpful advice for finding executive recruiters using Boolean search and for finding their emails using the free Chrome extension Hunter https://hunter.io.

The best way to connect with a search firm is to find someone working at the firm who you know. When the time is right, you can send them a short email letting them know you are ready to look. Attach your resume and see how they respond. In the worst case, if you don't hear back from them, you have been placed in their database, which is where they search for candidates first.

Here is an example of a short email or LI Message when you know someone, and they know you.

Subject: Hi from Dan Schwartz

Hi Herb

Good morning. I hope this finds you well and keeping busy.

Searching For A Job Sucks!

After five years at XYZ, a $100M enterprise software company, as a Director of Software Engineering, I have decided to start looking for a new opportunity:

- *VP of Software Engineering or CTO*

- *Small or mid-sized tech company*

- *Prefer the Mid-Atlantic*

- *Can also work remotely and travel as necessary.*

I'd enjoy catching up and discussing my search. Otherwise, please let me know if you see the right opportunity. My resume is attached.

I look forward to staying in touch and providing updates on my progress. If you have any open roles where access to my network would be helpful, let me know. I am happy to make an introduction. I am also happy to connect via LinkedIn, so you have access to my network of highly talented colleagues.

Thanks again,

Dan Schwartz

If you unpack this note, you'll notice five essential points.

1. It is short.

2. Bullets make it a quick and easy read.

3. It's clear about what I'd like to do next.

4. It offers a commitment to stay in touch.

CHAPTER 2: SEARCH - The Job Board Abyss

5. It offers help.

A warm introduction is the next best way to connect to a search firm or recruiter. If you can reference someone a recruiter has worked with in the past, they are more likely to respond. It may be more of a courtesy, but you will make a connection.

The email or LinkedIn message you send is like the preceding email but with a slight twist.

Subject: Referral from Barb Ryan

Hi Herb,

Good morning. My name is Dan Schwartz, and Barb Ryan, who you worked with on the Director of IT search for ABC, suggested I reach out to you. I have worked with Barb and have known her for years.

I am currently the Director of Software Engineering at XYZ, a $500M, highly successful international gaming company. After 5 years of great success with double-digit growth, I have decided to start looking for a new opportunity. I'd like to find the following:

- *VP of Software Engineering or CTO*
- *Small or mid-sized tech company*
- *Prefer Mid-Atlantic*
- *Can also work remotely and travel as necessary.*

Searching For A Job Sucks!

I would appreciate an introductory call to discuss my search. Otherwise, please let me know when you see the right opportunity. My resume is attached.

I look forward to staying in touch and providing updates on my progress. If you have any open roles where access to my network would be helpful, let me know. I am happy to make an introduction.

Thanks again,

Dan

While similar, this email is a little less warm. However, having a referral increases the odds that someone will respond.

And finally, when you don't have a personal connection or a warm referral, you are left with reaching out cold. Reaching out cold has the least chance of success, but it's the only option to get on their radar.

Most people think the best way to make this connection is to reach out to a senior-level person at the search firm. While that is certainly an option, another way is to reach out to the people whose job is to find people. Partners and vice presidents are not the ones doing this work. The people doing the work of finding people have titles like Researcher, Talent Acquisition Specialist, or Consultant. Depending on the firm, you may discover who they are by visiting the company website. You can also find them on LinkedIn.

These are the people who put together the list of prospects the search firm will contact. Being on their radar and staying in touch will keep you top of your mind if and when the right opportunity comes along.

Your email or LinkedIn message must grab the reader's attention quickly to receive a response.

Subject: Outstanding VP of Engineering candidate

Hi Herb

Good morning. My name is Dan Schwartz, and I am a Director of Software Engineering at XYZ company. XYZ is a $1B international company in the enterprise software industry with 5,000 employees.

After five years at XYZ, I have decided to seek a new opportunity. I am searching for the following:

- *VP of Software Engineering or CTO*
- *Small to mid-sized tech company*
- *Prefer Mid-Atlantic*
- *Can also work remotely and travel as necessary*

I would appreciate an introductory call to discuss my search. Otherwise, please let me know if you see the right opportunity. My resume is attached

I look forward to staying in touch and providing updates on my progress. If you have any open roles where access to my network would be helpful, let me know. I am happy to make an introduction.

I am also happy to provide referrals for open positions you are working to fill.

Thanks again,

Searching For A Job Sucks!

Dan

There is no question that this is a long shot, but if someone gets back to you, it is important to follow up with them regularly, so you stay on the search consultant's radar.

I often get asked how many consultants I need to contact at the same search firm. Once you reach out to one person, that's all you need. Once you share your resume, and if they consider you worthwhile, you are in their database and you can get called by anyone at the firm. Constantly reaching out and contacting multiple people isn't helpful, can be annoying, and smells of desperation.

If it sounds like you are doing all the work to establish a relationship and make it work, you are. Unfortunately, this is one relationship where you have very little control. When a search consultant identifies you as someone they value, you'll have a connection you'll want to hang on to for the life of your career.

While the odds of that happening are not high, if it does, consider yourself one of the lucky ones and don't screw it up. Don't take it for granted when a recruiter offers to introduce you to one of their colleagues or clients. Whenever they do this, they are putting their reputation in your hands. How you present yourself reflects on them. To preserve your relationship with the recruiter, you need to present yourself in the best professional light possible.

With that in mind, here are ways you can turn off your recruiter:

- Agreeing to an interview time and at the very last minute having to cancel. Other than illness or a death in the family, or your boss needs you immediately, if you've committed to be there, you better show up.

- Ghosting a scheduled interview and disappearing. It is hard to imagine why anyone would do this and risk ruining their reputation, but it happens.

- Continually calling a recruiter you've worked with in the past to see what's up. Most recruiters don't have time for general updates or chitchat.

- Asking your recruiter about posts on their Facebook page. Creepy. Recognize the difference between a personal relationship and a professional relationship. You are not trying to become best friends.

- Lying about anything at any time. Your recruiter needs to know everything, even if you think it might potentially hurt you. You need to be honest for them to help you. I can guarantee the relationship will be over if you get caught in a lie.

- Not telling the recruiter about other job search activity. If you are interviewing with other companies, tell the search firm. If they know this, they can try to influence the process.

- Complaining about your former boss or colleagues at any time during the process. Most recruiters view this as an immediate red flag.

- Blowing off your recruiter's phone calls, emails, or text messages.

Searching For A Job Sucks!

- Continually bugging the recruiter for an update after an interview. Following up with an email or phone call every week is adequate. More than that becomes annoying.

- Reaching out to a client directly after a recruiter has introduced you. The client has engaged the recruiter for a reason, so you must respect that relationship.

- Ignoring feedback. If your recruiter tells you something to do differently—listen! Don't act like you know more about the hiring process than they do.

- Disappearing after receiving a job offer. It may be hard to believe but this actually happens.

- Acting indignant after being rejected and writing your recruiter an angry email. There are many reasons why someone isn't selected. Don't assume it's all about you.

I speak to many candidates and quickly forget those who don't follow these guidelines. Your relationship with a recruiter can take years to establish, and it can be over in an instant.

When you do get called by a recruiter, there are a number of questions you'll want to ask. Having questions not only makes a good impression, but they also help turn the interview into a conversation which is always your goal. Caroline Castrillon published "10 Questions to Ask a Recruiter During a Job Interview" for Forbes.

- What does the interview process look like?

- Is this a new role or an existing position?

- What qualities do you look for in new hires?

- To whom would I report, and what can you tell me about them?

- Can you tell me more about the role?

- What is the salary range for the job?

- How would you describe the company culture?

- How would you describe the team I would be working with?

- How does the company support career development and advancement?

- Do you have any concerns about my qualifications?

There is another side to this relationship that also deserves attention. You, too, have a choice in this relationship, and just because a recruiter calls you and shows interest doesn't mean you need to reciprocate. Use the following checklist to evaluate your experience with a recruiter. If you feel uncomfortable, you have the right to cancel the relationship.

- Does the recruiter have a signed agreement with the client?

- If the relationship isn't retained, is it exclusive?

- Does the recruiter provide accurate and detailed information about the job and the company early in the process?

Searching For A Job Sucks!

- Does the recruiter do an excellent job explaining the recruitment process from start to finish and how long the process will take?

- Does the recruiter set clear expectations for compensation early in the process?

- Does the recruiter show interest in your background and make you feel appreciated as you progress?

- Does the recruiter understand your industry?

- Does the recruiter provide updates, behave honestly, and stay in touch during the recruitment process?

- Does the recruiter adequately prepare you for interviews?

- Would you recommend this recruiter to a close professional colleague or friend?

All recruiters operate differently, so putting a quality filter on your experience is essential. If the relationship doesn't feel right, it isn't, and it's time to move on. On the other hand, if you feel a great connection and find their advice and counsel helpful, you'll want to stay as close to this relationship for as long as you can.

Key Messages

Working with Search firms isn't easy. You need to do all of the work to make the relationship work. When you make a connection with a search consultant, ideally before you need them, it's important to hold onto them. Regularly touching base to be helpful builds a connection that will hopefully pay dividends in the future.

If a search consultant doesn't get back to you, don't take it personally or assume they are no longer interested. Remember, search firms don't work for you; they work for their client who is paying the bill.

The same is true for internal recruiters at organizations where you'd like to work. Keep in touch and be useful.

Research external firms to make sure they place people in your industry and discipline. You have limited time so spend it where there is the greatest chance of success.

Search firms are an important part of your job search game plan but don't spend more than 20% of your time chasing them down. Focusing on building an army of people that want to help you find that next opportunity.

Coaching Questions

- Who are the search firms that place people in your industry or discipline?

- Who are the search consultants you've spoken to the past that you haven't reached out to in the last 3 to 4 months?

- When was the last time you ask a colleague in your industry or discipline what search consultants they know, respect and trust?

Searching For A Job Sucks!

It's More Than Who You Know; It's All about Relationships

Since publishing my first book, How to Find a New Job Without Looking: Building Vital Relationships That Lead to a Successful Career, which is available on Amazon, I have spoken to hundreds of people about My Vital Few™ and the importance of relationships. Your My Vital Few™ are your most important and valued personal and professional connections. I can't say it often enough, the success of your career will often be measured by the people you meet and the relationships you build on your journey. You can't do this alone; we all need help. And the more you offer help to others, the more you can expect in return. That is the essence of networking as a lifestyle and what building, maintaining and nurturing relationships is all about. The book provides examples, templates, and messaging to put this way of operating into practice. It doesn't matter if you are 21 or 61, you will find it is never too early or too late to get started.

For those of you wondering why I am so adamant about networking as a lifestyle, read what others have reported. The *Journal of Energy Management* in 2024 reported, "According to Hub Spot, 85% of jobs are filled through networking." In fact, according to CNBC, "70% of jobs are never posted publicly." This same article references a study by Oxford Economics that demonstrated "Networking not only helps you start a career but also helps you succeed at it."

According to Top Resume "A majority of job postings are not available online, with 60 percent of jobs being found through networking instead. The same article also reported that 75% of resumes are rejected before they reach the hiring manager."

In a 2020 survey from LinkedIn, "73% of respondents were hired as a result of someone they know making an introduction or a connection. Another 70% had a personal connection to someone in the company." A 2022 survey noted that "42% of professionals found their current jobs through some form or effect of networking."

Another 2023 study recently found that a user's "weak ties" on LinkedIn can increase job transmission and impact job mobility—even more than stronger, closer connections."

While the numbers may vary, they all point to why you hear so much about networking as the way to tap into the "hidden job market." In many respects, for many professionals, and especially anyone with a director level title or above, tapping into the hidden job marketing isn't a choice. For a variety of reasons, many jobs are kept confidential, so stop expecting to find them posted on a job board. In fact, a *Wall Street Journal* article by Callum Borchers and Lindsay Ellis says it all in its title: "Landing a Job Is All About Who You Know (Again)." The article went on to note that "the key to finding a new position often turns on a personal connection that can pluck your resume out of online obscurity and ensure it has been seen by a real person.

Even with that evidence, the employment agency Apollo Technical reported while "79% of professionals agree that networking is valuable for career progression, according to LinkedIn, only 48% consistently keep in touch with their network." The main reason for this is not having enough time. Anyone who knows me well, knows I never buy "not having enough time" as an excuse. We all have all the time we need to do whatever matters most. When someone tells me they don't have time to invest in their My Vital Few™, it is another way of saying it isn't a priority. While I must respect their choice, they clearly don't understand the cost associated with that decision.

Ironically, these are the same people who approach me after getting laid off, or for one reason or another, are unhappy in their current job. The fact that you have to "search" is where the problem begins. Remember, the people who are the best at staying in touch with their My Vital Few™ rarely find themselves in this position. The jobs find them. You know these people. These are the ones who land in a new job, and you comment to yourself "I didn't know they were looking." I don't care if you call this precious group of relationships your My Vital Few™ or your Kitchen Cabinet; these are relationships you never want to neglect. These are the people who will potentially have the biggest impact on your career.

So, What Can You Do?

While I can't review all of the strategies and tactics covered in my first book, I do want to share four questions I recommend job seekers make part of their informational interviewing and job-seeking process. These questions keep the process moving and get you closer to your desired outcome. When you reframe networking as I do in my book, it is more about building long-lasting relationships than necessarily finding a job. In fact, done well, networking as a lifestyle extends well beyond looking for a job. It's what you do every day when you meet people and how you interact with them.

Here are the four questions:

1. Who do you know who might have some advice on the market, my resume, my job search strategy, and so on?

2. What recruiters have you worked with in the past whom you like and respect?

3. Can I follow up with you in a few weeks and give you an update on my progress?

4. How can I help you? For example, I've been learning a lot about XYZ in my job search—would that be helpful to share?

Notice what I didn't do. I didn't ask for a job. The odds of someone having the perfect job when you meet with them are almost nonexistent. Knowing that, why would you put someone on the spot and make them feel uncomfortable by asking the question? Of course, you wouldn't. Ask questions the person can likely answer. If they agreed to meet, they obviously want to be helpful—don't make that hard for them. If, and when, the relationship evolves, you'll get the chance to ask more difficult questions.

If you are reading this chapter and find yourself getting uncomfortable about the idea of networking, not to worry. Just because you may be more of an introvert, doesn't mean you can't be great at this most critical skill. My advice is to be yourself and find ways that work best for you. I am an introvert, so the way I network looks different from others.

There are 10 possible answers to this dilemma that are worth considering. At the moment, I can only think of 9.

Searching For A Job Sucks!

1. Forget about networking. What? I thought you just said.... I did, but networking to many people sounds scary and intimidating. Focus more on getting to know people and building relationships. We are social creatures and crave interaction and connection.

2. It's about quality, not quantity. How many people can you actually get to know that well? Take the pressure off yourself. Focus on people one at a time regardless of how many are in the proverbial room. Find people where you feel a relationship based on mutual interests, shared experiences, and a personal connection. These may become your My Vital Few™. You may have several thousand LinkedIn connections, but only a handful of those really matter. In fact, I no longer think of LinkedIn as a networking tool. I think of it as a database where I can find useful information. Once I find what I need, I jump out as quickly as I can, so I don't get distracted by all the noise.

3. Email and phone. If the idea of going to mixers or association/industry events causes you to break out in hives, much of what I'm describing can be accomplished via email and phone calls. Craft an email like the ones I've shared and ask to make a connection. You can then follow up with a phone call and have the conversation. While I always encourage face-to-face meetings, or even video meetings, email and phone can work.

4. Ask questions and be curious. If striking up a conversation is difficult, try asking questions. For example: What are you working on? Why do you enjoy that work? What are your

current projects? What's your experience with *XYZ*? How about those Yankees? Be curious about the other person and focus less on yourself. When the conversation eventually turns to you, you will feel more comfortable because you know something about the person you are speaking to.

5. Listen and learn. Often times when we think of networking, we think of people who know how to work the room. They do all the talking and try to impress people with all they know. The best networkers I know spend more time listening than talking. How can you understand someone's problem, or if they are struggling and need assistance unless you are listening?

6. Offer to help. As you ask questions and listen, you may eventually arrive at a place where you can offer to help. Many people who are intentionally engaged in networking focus on what they need and forget that the secret to relationship building is what you can offer, not what you receive.

7. Be opportunistic. Pay attention to what is happening in the moment and the chance to make a connection when you least expect it. Every meeting, every chance encounter is an opportunity to build a relationship. When you sense a connection or opportunity, lean in and see how for it goes.

8. Social media. Make it easier for people to find you by being active on LinkedIn. You can post, comment on posts, and even write an article. You can show the world your expertise without bragging. The more people know about you, the more

they will reach out to you, and the less you will have to reach out to them.

9. Follow up. Many people reach out to me for help with their job search. After spending 30 minutes with them, sharing everything I can to help with their search, I never hear back from them. Maybe they didn't find the conversation helpful? I suppose that's possible. Or, maybe they are falling into the one-and-done trap that I see over and over. If you follow up at some regular interval, I will remember you. If you don't, you will likely be forgotten. That may be okay from your perspective, and I won't take it personally. If not, you are missing a potential opportunity to stay in touch with someone who may be able to help. The other reason follow-up is important is to pay it forward. How can you extend an offer to help if you never circle back to the person who was helpful.

I don't like ending with an odd number, so here is the other reason and perhaps the most important. This gets at the heart of what networking is all about.

10. Pay it forward. The other reason follow-up is important is to pay it forward. How can you extend an offer to help if you never circle back?

Informational interviews are one of the most common strategies for starting the relationship-building process. While often associated with searching for a job, they are also a great way to get to know people. Ultimately, you hope it might lead to an opportunity in the future, but that only happens if you make a positive impression. I cover this extensively in my first book.

I'll leave you here with a challenge. Almost daily you can find an article on LinkedIn that talks about how to improve your job search. In the spirit of process improvement, why spend time trying to improve a flawed process. Your goal should be to eliminate the need for a job search altogether. I can't say this often enough, loud enough or any other way, focus on building, maintaining, and nurturing relationships. The more you demonstrate care, compassion, and genuine concern for others, the more you will experience in return. Do more listening than speaking. In fact, listening to understand versus listening to respond may be the most important skill you will ever learn. My friend Kingsley Akins says, "hard skills" get you on the career ladder, "soft skills" get you up the career ladder." Be viewed as someone who "offers" rather than "asks." You will be amazed at the opportunities that come your direction.

Key Messages

More and more I'm telling people it takes an army to find a job. Go build an army of people willing to help in any way they can. Find everyone who is willing to provide input, advice, support, suggestions, referrals and connections. Build an army of people who are working on your behalf and keep in regular contact. You can find a Networking Guide and Tracker at https://billfitzgerald.biz that will make that easy to do.

Most people are willing to help. Make it easy for them. Just give them the opportunity. The people who do the most are your My Vital Few™. Never let them get away. This is how you pay it forward

Searching For A Job Sucks!

when they need assistance. That's what networking is all about. It's not what you get, it's what you give.

Make the four questions part of the conversations you have with people. You may not ask each question every time, but they will generate a wealth of knowledge to help with your search and longer after.

And not to sound too self-serving, read my book *How to Find a New Job Without Looking: Building Vital Relationships That Lead to a Successful Career*, so you never have to search for a job.

Coaching Questions

- What prevents you from networking more and how do you overcome that obstacle?

- Do you know who is in your army?

- How often do you pay it forward?

CHAPTER 2: SEARCH - The Job Board Abyss

If You Are 50, You Are Now Considered Old

Searching for a job at any time in your life when you are unemployed can be a very lonely and scary place. Most days, you can't see an end to your job-search misery. No matter what you try, nothing seems to work. You begin to wonder what the people in your network think when you continue to reach out for help. When you apply for a job online, you rarely hear anything. The recruiters you speak to say you are great and never follow up or return your calls.

This experience is especially common for people over 50. That may be politically incorrect to say aloud, but let's be honest, that is what people talk about in private and believe to be reality. In fact, there is research published by AARP that reports in an online article "Age Discrimination Among Workers Age 50+" that indicates "about two in three adults ages 50-plus in the labor force (64%) think older workers face age discrimination in the workplace today. And among them, nearly all (90%) believe that age discrimination against older workers is common in the workplace." If you still have questions about the presence of age discrimination, talk to people you know and you will hear firsthand how age discrimination shows itself in the hiring process.

As if you need additional evidence to acknowledge the presence and impact of age discrimination, there is a very scientific study, published in 2023 by the University of California Press and titled "Ageism in Hiring: A Systematic Review and Meta-analysis of Age Discrimination."

I know from firsthand experience that there are times when hiring managers want younger people and are very explicit about the request. There are circumstances where that makes sense, and other times, well, you decide. When a client says I need someone with runway they aren't talking about the airport.

Most recently, I hear this cry a lot from white males over 50. I don't say this to generate sympathy for white males over 50. White males over 50 have had the upper hand forever. The fact is, times have changed, so get over it and adjust. We finally see and embrace the value that many aspects of diversity—experience, thinking, background—can bring to our organizations. Smart organizations are doing all they can to build companies that attract and retain the very best talent in the marketplace. White males over 50, while still valuable, no longer represent only the best of what is available. I also believe the pendulum has tipped too far in one direction to correct past wrongs and to ensure greater equity. Eventually, I believe that will tilt back to a new normal, to whatever that looks like for this marketplace; but in the meantime, for some people, especially those over 50, it makes searching for a job almost impossible. I'm not suggesting the only reason people over 50 can't find a job is because they are over 50. If I'm keeping it real, however, that is one of the reasons.

In my experience, there is at least one reason why companies often prefer to hire younger people, and that has to do with succession. If you can hire someone with more years left in their career, you don't have to hire again for the foreseeable future. Generally speaking, the preference is to hire someone who can stay and grow with the company. Not that you necessarily can't if you are over 50, but that is the stereotype you are fighting.

The other reality that comes with age is relevancy. The older you get, the more your background and experience is dated and perhaps not as relevant to today's problems and opportunities. Technology is moving quickly, and you need to keep up with new ways of working and solving problems. The learning curve for someone who has grown up in the digital world is much shorter. The bias is to find people who will introduce new technology and ways of working to the organization. While it isn't true for everyone, the perception of someone over 50 is these candidates are less inclined to have that ability. They may have other capabilities, but this is the one that matters most.

I often hear older job seekers say their age and experience will help them coach younger professionals so they can be more successful. You may think that is the case, but what matters in this marketplace is expertise. Truth is, organizations talk a good game about the importance of people, but if quarterly or yearly numbers aren't meeting expectations or if future guidance indicates leaner times, organizations will downsize in a heartbeat. We are seeing that now with many tech firms announcing hundreds, if not thousands, of layoffs.

So, What Can You Do?

How many of you have heard the dreaded word *overqualified*? That can often be code for too old. There may also be a fear that you might be bored and quit. Or, that you leave as soon as you are offered something more senior or that pays more. I'm sure this fear exists because some hiring manager has had this experience. You need to handle this objection in a way that alleviates any fear you are a flight risk.

Searching For A Job Sucks!

If the job you are applying for is an obvious step back, it is best to be upfront and acknowledge that reality (it's what they are thinking, so address it while you have the chance), but that you have a reason for being interested. For example:

- This is an opportunity to do interesting work and make a difference without the responsibility of leading people.

- This is a bridge of 5, 7, to 10 years before you retire.

- This is work you enjoy and plays to your strengths.

- You aren't ready to retire and enjoy working.

The key is to address the potential objections upfront and provide an answer that makes sense and helps the hiring manager solve their problem—finding and hiring a highly talented individual to fill their open position.

I don't want to be a pessimist, but there is one reality you can't change. If individuals or organizations are predisposed to only hire younger professionals or to engage in blatant discrimination, there is very little you can do unless you want to incur the time and expense to file a lawsuit. To me, that is valuable time you can never get back and you might be better off working on your job search. It has proven difficult to win age discrimination cases in court. Cilenti & Cooper is a law firm in New York that protects employees from unlawful discrimination. It states that "ageism is harder to prove because it is subtle and hard to recognize." This is clearly a difficult path to pursue, so what else can you do?

I recently read an article by Amanda Augustine titled "7 Signs Your Resume Is Making You Look Old." Amanda offered worthwhile tips to get your foot in the door.

- Your resume is too long.

- You still use an AOL email account.

- The phone number of your resume is your landline.

- You still include entry-level jobs from 30 years ago.

- You have two spaces at the end of a sentence—this means you learned to type on a typewriter.

- You have an objectives statement as opposed to a Professional Summary.

- You didn't include a link to your LinkedIn profile.

These are all good points to apply to your resume. These might help you get past the first hurdle. Unfortunately, once you get to the step where you are in a face-to-face meeting, either in person or over a Zoom call, you won't be able to hide your age any longer. If you don't get passed to the next stage of the interviewing process, the vague feedback you'll hear is "not a good fit." That is often code for too old. What else do you expect them to say? "I'm going to pass because I prefer to hire someone younger, around 35." It is to their advantage to be vague and not risk a potential legal action based on age discrimination.

I also believe it is important to listen to yourself talk and the words you choose.

Searching For A Job Sucks!

Telling stories that start with "back in the day" or "years ago" or "before the internet was around" or "when I started working" signal someone may be older than what you want to appear.

I believe it is okay to say you have 10, 20, or even 30 years of experience so long as you mention "with progressive leadership roles in x, y, or z and demonstrated accomplishment" or with a "demonstrated record of accomplishments and advancement."

Nowadays, communication occurs via Zoom, Slack, or collaboration tools like Microsoft Teams. Referencing a fax machine makes you sound dated.

Don't mention basic computer skills like MS Office on your resume. It's okay to mention more current tools like Trello or Kanban or Google Chat.

Rather than "To whom it may concern," try using "Dear Mr./Ms. (Hiring Manager Name)."

If you have worked the same job search strategy for months without success, and this applies to everyone, not just people over 50, why are you expecting a different outcome? The market is telling you something; I just don't know if you want to hear the message. The harsh reality may require you to recalibrate your expectations. Maybe you need to look at lower-level jobs, perhaps you need to look at organizations that aren't as well-known and prestigious, and if you aren't able to retire, maybe you need to make a lifestyle adjustment so you don't need to earn as much.

Hearing this isn't easy, but maybe it's time.

If you find yourself in this place, I can offer one piece of advice that aligns with our current marketplace. Here it is: it is time to redefine your area of expertise and focus your search on something more realistic and attainable.

Over the years, the market has shifted to an expertise-driven economy. When you hear all the talk about defining your brand, this is what all the fancy talk is referring to. You need to capture what you are great at doing. Stated another way, what can you do aside from watching others do what they do? For example, I may be the CEO of an executive search firm, but I would speak to my ability to find people, recruit them, screen them, and help close them.

There was a time when your ability to lead and be a good manager was highly valued. Most managers are now expected to be an individual contributor while simultaneously managing a team of people. Look at what people get rewarded for at work. They get rewarded for what they do, not for helping others be successful. That's sad to say, but that is the reality in many organizations.

If you have spent years building a management- or executive-level career and are struggling to find a job, it may be time to reframe who you are. A CEO (chief executive officer), COO (chief operating officer), CMO (chief marketing officer), CFO (chief financial officer), CRO (chief revenue officer), VP (Vice President), or Director role may no longer be in your future. Instead, it's time to focus on whatever technical or functional skills you can offer and highlight those more than anything else. So, rather than lead, what can you do that will help get work done?

Searching For A Job Sucks!

I often hear older workers argue that they can bring a level of maturity and wisdom to the workplace. No one cares. If they did, you wouldn't get laid off. It's what you can do that matters.

Figure out what you are great at and what problems you can solve. What does the market value? Listen to what the market is telling you, target a specific audience, and let people know you are looking.

The second piece of advice I often give to older job seekers, once they know what they want to do, is to start building a network. With all the obstacles to getting hired that we've mentioned, I believe the greatest chance of success is building relationships that can help you find the right opportunity. My first book, *How to Find a New Job Without Looking*, outlined in detail the process for making that happen. The reason I wrote an entire book on that one topic is because I know from years of experience and working with thousands of job seekers that it works. If you are over 50 and have never considered this strategy, it is time to use it, and it can still work.

To start building your network, I highly encourage you to embrace a strategy I call referrals, recommendations, and references. If you are over 50, this may be your greatest chance at finding a job.

1. Referrals are from people you may not know very well or even at all, but they want to be helpful. The likelihood of this increases if there is some common experience—you attended the same school or share a common interest.

2. Recommendations are from people you know and likely know very well. These people can offer whole-hearted endorsements based on past experience working with you.

Referrals and recommendations hopefully get you introduced to someone who can get your resume into the right hands. To achieve that will require some serious research and outreach. Consider the following:

- Who do you know or whom are you connected to that works at the organization where you'd like to apply?

- Who do you know or whom are you connected to that used to work at the organization where you'd like to apply?

- Who can you find on LinkedIn that attended your alma mater that works at the organization where you'd like to apply?

- Who is a manager in the appropriate department at the organization where you would like to apply?

Use the LinkedIn search filters to find people that closely align with your background.

Once you find them, use the templates provided in the book to reach out.

3. References are part of the hiring process, but these are likely former bosses who can speak directly to your capability and work ethic. Recruiters will likely ask you for three, but the ones that carry the most weight are former bosses. Who you choose may depend on the role, but you can ask people in advance, so they are ready to go.

Searching For A Job Sucks!

My third piece of advice is to apply what you learned in the chapter about writing a resume and focus on the results, outcomes, and performance that matter most to each employer. This requires some research, but they need to see you have the experience and ability to solve their problem. If you can take away my pain, you are more likely to get my attention. This is how entrepreneurs think. Entrepreneurs are focused on problems and how they can make life at work or at home easier. Think of yourself as an entrepreneur and focus on business problems you can solve.

My fourth piece of advice is to target organizations that have made a commitment to hiring older workers. AARP (formerly the American Association of Retired Persons) has a list of over 1,000 organizations that have taken a pledge to hire older workers. These organizations are all over the country and represent many different industries. The AARP list is a resource worth checking out. Once you find that perfect organization, it's time to focus on the expertise you can bring and to utilize the referral, recommendation, and reference strategy to get your foot in the door.

My last piece of advice is to not give up. As discouraging as it may get, find people who can support you on this journey. Support is both empathy and accountability. Find someone who can listen and encourage and validate all you offer, but who will also keep pushing and not let you feel sorry for yourself. I truly believe there is a home for everyone. You just need to be realistic about what you can expect. The market doesn't lie, so use the feedback to evaluate your approach and expectations.

CHAPTER 2: SEARCH - The Job Board Abyss

Key Messages

Finding a job as you get older becomes harder. The fact is that age discrimination is real and something you have to deal with. You need to reframe your age as an advantage and point to all you know and how you can contribute. Specifically, focus on what you can do as an individual contributor as opposed to a senior level executive. Take the time to learn new skills or refresh old ones. Organizations look for people that can get stuff done. Not people who watch people getting stuff done.

When organizations and hiring managers are predisposed to discriminate, there is very little you can do. Walk away and find places where your experience will be valued.

For those over 50, building and leveraging your network is going to be your greatest key to success. If there were ever a time to build an army of supportive people who want to help you, it is now.

For some, this period in your life may require a recalibration of lifestyle and expenses. That can remove some of the anxiety associated with having to find a job.

Coaching Questions

- What can you change about your current job search strategy to increase your odds of success?

- Do you present yourself as someone who can do things?

- How much anxiety does your current lifestyle and monthly expenses create and is it time to make a change?

Searching For A Job Sucks!

Lessons from Job Seekers

Think Strategically

Karl is a 48-year-old individual contributor salesperson who has been in the same industry for about 27 years. He has a great track record of success and is viewed as an industry expert by many people who know him.

His last company was the best he had ever worked for, and he did incredibly well. He had great support from the top, and the culture was extremely healthy and collaborative. The company did well, growing every year, and he established relationships with very high-profile customers in the industry. He was challenged to bring in new partners and help existing partners be successful.

There was a major change when the beloved CEO was pushed out by the board and replaced. Since then, many C-level executives have departed. Karl planned to stay on to see how everything played out, but after his boss resigned that changed everything.

Karl started to become concerned and decided he had had enough. He started looking in January and his search lasted about three months. Karl stayed with the company while he was looking. He emphatically made the point that finding a new job is easier to find a job when you have a job.

He believes he was successful at finding a job because of networking. He reached out to his network, which included a former leader of Karl's current company who had started a new job. This person is well-connected in their industry and introduced Karl to a close friend and colleague who happened to work for a competitor in the industry.

Karl met with this person and had a great conversation. It turns out there was a position open at the company. This person referred Karl to another person in the company for a conversation. This person decided Karl would be a great fit and asked him to apply formally and to use her name as an internal reference.

Karl heard from a recruiter very quickly and had several rounds of interviews, and eventually, was offered a job.

Karl had interviews with other companies, but he didn't know people on the inside. In one case, he had an interview and was told to expect to hear back for another interview. He sent thank you notes and never heard anything. He asked if he was still being considered and no one ever got back to him.

Karl kept a detailed spread sheet to keep track of contacts, conversations, follow-up dates, and so on. As a result, he has grown and expanded his network and believes he is well positioned for the future.

He also worked with someone on his resume and was really happy with the outcome. After getting his resume updated, he had more bites. That said, in this market, Karl believes it's who you know that makes the difference. It would have taken a lot longer had he not used his network to his advantage.

Karl believes it's a waste of time to apply without knowing someone.

Mass applying doesn't work.

Searching For A Job Sucks!

It's frustrating to apply for a position that feels like an ideal fit, customize your cover letter, and resume, and never hear anything. Not having a personal connection on the inside seemed to be the deciding factor. In the future, he will be far more strategic and not waste his time when he doesn't have a referral.

There is an inverse relationship between the number of jobs you apply for and your level of frustration. Applying for lots of jobs only increases your level of frustration. Spray and pray is not a good job search strategy.

Karl spent a lot of time asking for introductions. He has created relationships that he can reach out to in the future for a variety of reasons beyond looking for job. Karl understands it will be important to stay in touch with these folks on a regular basis for three reasons:

1. He can be there when they need assistance.

2. They will return his call when he needs assistance.

3. When these close connections hear about a great career opportunity, he is the first person they think of.

Karl's advice is to use your network, ask for introductions, and maintain contact with people. Thank them for their time, check in, build rapport, talk shop. Know whom you are talking to ahead of time and what they are up to.

When someone offers you a referral, ask the person making the referral to tell you something about them. Know whom you are talking to ahead of time and what they are up to. Knowing this makes the path to building rapport much easier.

Technology Isn't Always Your Friend

Carol is a 65-year-old technical writer who writes software documentation. She has been in that field 27 years and has been a high-level individual contributor most of her career. Carol was part of a mass layoff that happened unexpectedly at a large technology company.

The people in her group were told the company needed different skills, but they found their jobs posted in other countries. She had only been there a year and a half, so it was very shocking. She had been laid off from her previous position after two-and-one-half years, which was also a surprise. In the past five years, she had two layoffs in her 60s. Prior to that, she had never been laid off in her career and that included the 2008 Lehman stock crash.

Carol landed at another company that is a subsidiary of a Japanese conglomerate, which has been in business 91 years. The products include software and hardware with a focus on agriculture and infrastructure. She had started her career in a related industry, so when she applied online, she had an edge.

She looked for a new job for about five months but that was over the Thanksgiving, Christmas, and New Year's holidays when not as much happens. The last time she was laid off, two years before, it took three months to land a new job and it wasn't that difficult. She hit Easy Apply on LinkedIn and eventually was hired into her best job ever. She was disappointed and angry when she was laid off this time, but wasn't worried.

Searching For A Job Sucks!

Carol describes the experience this time as difficult and traumatic. Before January, she had applied for 90 jobs on LinkedIn, 20 of those were contract jobs, which she started to apply to when she wasn't getting traction on full-time roles and needed to consider contract jobs. Out of the 90, about 60 never responded; she heard from 30 that were either rejections, or an interview, or a question about compensation.

She found her current job when it was posted on LinkedIn in early January and saw something in the posting that asked for a unique skill Carol has in her background. She immediately applied and messaged the recruiter. After three to four weeks, the recruiter circled back to schedule a call. Carol commented that it seems to take forever when you are unemployed and looking for a job. When she looks back, in her case, it didn't take any longer than when she was employed and looking. It was her level of anxiety and the pressure she felt that made the experience seem much slower.

Carol was very aware of the emotional aspect of not working. There is no outlet for reward and productivity and camaraderie. You are out of your routine; there is only negative reward because you are being rejected and it starts to eat away at your confidence level. You start to ask yourself, "What's wrong with me?" If you love what you do and it is taken away, you've lost a part of you that is important to who you are.

She went through her 200 contacts and didn't find people that could help her. She also had no interest in starting to attend events and schmooze with people she really didn't care to get to know.

Most challenging for her was keeping up the momentum after doing everything she thought she should do and not seeing results. She structured her day, created a to-do list, learned about keyword matching to update her resume. In retrospect, she didn't really see much value in the keyword exercise. By month four, she was feeling burned out by the process, which was scary. She wonders what happens to other people when they give up.

Carol found the digital hiring process frustrating because there is no response after you apply. Or you get rejected before you've even had any human contact. Your resume gets scanned for keywords, and there are many applicants for most jobs. With more remote opportunities, you are now competing with people all over the world.

Carol also realized she never tapped into the recruiting marketplace to find recruiters who could have been working for her. In retrospect, she would have done the research to find recruiters in her industry who could get her access to new opportunities. She believes that she and her colleagues suffered every single day exposing themselves to the LinkedIn platform that is basically designed to beat them up and spit them out of the process.

Looking back, what worked in her search was having a support group—the people she had worked with that had also been laid off. They met together weekly for months. They shared jobs together and they wanted to help each other. It felt like they were working together to increase their odds of getting hired. If someone didn't see a job, someone else in the group would bring it to the others' attention. They have thought about meeting once a month and bringing back people who have found jobs. She realizes that her hundreds of LinkedIn connections will never provide this level of intimacy and support. For that reason, she wants to stay in touch with them, and at minimum, pay it forward if someone else in the group needs assistance. This group became her lifeline.

She believes she wasted lots of time on a LinkedIn, given the low return and that was true for many in her group. It worked better two years ago, but that must have been luck or karma. She would absolutely look for recruiters who could help her and stop trying to slay the LinkedIn dragon.

Don't Run from Something; Run to Something

Darren is a white male, 47 years old, and has been a recruiter most of his career. If anyone knows something about recruiting and hiring, this guy does!

Darren has mostly been an individual contributor and has worked for several large, well-known firms.

After 15 years at one of those large firms, Darren decided to leave because he wanted to try something different. He wasn't seeing the opportunity for advancement so decided to venture out.

With COVID, he saw the opportunity to look more remotely and connected with a tech start-up far away in San Diego. As the tech market started to slide in the fall of 2022, Darren was caught up in a layoff.

Darren looked for over two months before he found his next job. He made the point that he was very thoughtful about where he applied. He knows people who will apply for 100 jobs a month and views that as an absolute waste of time. He applied to 40 jobs over two months

CHAPTER 2: SEARCH - The Job Board Abyss

and spent lots of time researching the companies before applying. He would dig into their products and services, who works there, their financials, what positions are open, and so on.

Darren recognizes that companies make it easy to apply, but how do you stand out from the masses? Darren's advice: go direct. Avoid online applications and do all you can to find a warm introduction. Short of that, find creative ways to reach out to recruiters or hiring managers directly. Of the 40 jobs he applied for, he heard back from 12 and he had a handful of interviews.

What Darren found most challenging was the lack of communication when you apply. Often, you hear nothing. As a recruiter, Darren understands you don't have the capacity to reply to every applicant. While it feels lousy, he doesn't expect it to change, and job seekers need to set their expectations accordingly. Darren also sees job seekers pound the LinkedIn Easy Apply job button, and in those instances, they don't merit the time it takes to generate a response.

What annoyed him most about the process was uploading his resume online and have it not parsed correctly and having to start the application process over. It may not be intentional, but companies don't always make it easy to apply. That is the other reason to avoid online applications.

Darren kept a spreadsheet of his activity for unemployment purposes. Most people won't think of this, but it is a good reminder.

When it comes to interviewing, Darren was often shocked at how little the interviewers knew about his background. Someone asked him if he had any technical recruiting experience and that's all he has done his entire career. He tries to make his resume readable and easy to understand because he knows people don't spend a lot of time reading.

Ultimately, networking was Darren's key to finding another job. One of Darren's close connections was having coffee with a friend who asked if he knew any recruiters looking for work. Darren's friend made the introduction, and within two weeks, Darren was back to work.

Darren learned how important it is to research companies where he is interviewing. With so many opportunities remote, you likely won't know the companies as well. The key is knowing your audience: What are their challenges? What are they looking for? Is the interviewer the recruiter, the hiring manger, the HR person? He would have different questions for each person.

Darren didn't want to run away from something but wanted to run toward something. Looking back, he might have started his search earlier. It is easier to find a job when you have a job. You need to be thoughtful when you decide to make a move. You don't want to end up with the same crap in a different pig pen.

Finally, Darren advises that you do the necessary research on a company before you make a move. Don't make an ill-advised move and end up looking for another job in six months. While you may be unhappy in your current position, there is no guarantee that the next job will be any better. Learn as much as you can before taking the leap.

You Don't Have to Apply for Everything

Margaret is 35 years old and has spent all her career in politics as a professional campaign organizer. She has worked in this capacity for 12 years for several different organizations.

Margaret started looking for a job when she learned that a layoff was coming. She was told by Senior Management that her department wouldn't be affected, but she wanted to play it safe. Much to her surprise, she was part of the group impacted.

Her full-on job search lasted for two months. She spent about 25 hours a week dedicated to finding a new job.

Margaret hadn't interviewed in a while, so it was difficult getting back into the interviewing process and feeling comfortable. She was very successful at getting interviews, but it took many interviews to get the job she wanted.

For Margaret, the process is a slog. Writing another cover letter, another email, another application, and so on. Going through the same motions over and was painful.

Margaret found it frustrating to apply for a job she was highly overqualified for and not getting past the first round of interviews. She never knew why and was left wondering what she could do differently the next time.

She also found it disappointing to apply for jobs she thought were a great fit and never hear anything. This was true even when she had connections at the organization. It seems like organizations post jobs and they are not ready to hire. In the nonprofit world, the process is painfully slow.

She eventually found her new job by applying for a job she found on a niche job board. She finds these job boards more valuable than the large consumer boards.

Looking back on her job search, Margaret thought reaching out to people working in organizations where she applied online helped her a lot. In the case of her current organization, someone put in a good word about Margaret and her resume rose to the top. Leveraging connections helped her a great deal.

As a result of going through the process, she picked up good interviewing skills. When describing her experience, she learned to focus on the outcome first before diving into the detail. The recruiter was helpful in setting herself up for success.

If she had to do it over, she would have been more selective. She applied for some jobs she wasn't all that excited about and that was a waste of time. Margaret felt a level of urgency and thought applying to everything would relieve some of the anxiety. In truth, it only increased her level of anxiety.

If Margaret were to share any advice about searching for a job it would to be: treat your job search like a job and put in the time. Her mantra was apply, search, connect. You can't expect to get a job by applying to one job a week. Her goal was five jobs a week and any more was too much.

CHAPTER 2: SEARCH - The Job Board Abyss

What People Say and Think about You Matters

Darren is a 66-year-old technology sales executive. He has worked in the software industry his entire career and has an enviable track record of success.

Darren was looking for a new position because he was laid off from his previous job.

In total, Darren was looking for 4 months. He was laid off on a Friday and reached out to a former colleague on Monday. This former colleague happens to sit on the board of a company in the same industry where Darren had worked for years. This former colleague thought Darren would be a perfect fit for a senior sales role they needed to fill and couldn't believe he was available.

Darren went through the interviewing process meeting everyone on the team. The choice came down to Darren and one other guy. The other guy was someone the investors knew and liked, and that guy received the offer.

After returning from vacation, he started looking in earnest. He had a few different conversations but unexpectedly, the CEO from the first company called and said the other guy wasn't a good fit and wanted to know if he still might be interested. The conversations picked up again and they offered him the job. Darren was hoping to get a job through his network, and it worked out.

At his age, Darren knows ageism exists and it depends on the company and how much they value your experience. Your choices boil down to your network, LinkedIn, or other job boards. Darren considers networking to be the most valuable, but you can't rely just on that. He brushed up his LinkedIn profile and his resume to make a better appearance.

Darren found LinkedIn super frustrating. He'd look at jobs at the big tech companies and see 100 to 400 applications per job. He decided to broaden his search beyond the VP level to even Account Management roles. He was most interested in staying busy and working regardless of the level. At the same time Darren received the job offer he eventually accepted, he was going to receive an offer from another company. Surprising to Darren, that opportunity came from a job posting. He believes the only reason that worked was because the post was very specific about the niche technology they required. Darren's experience lined up perfectly with that requirement. In addition, the company was a startup and Darren grew up in that environment. He also had the required years of executive experience and exposure. It was very niche, and the post was highly specific which seemed to be the key.

Ultimately, what worked for Darren was his network and it was a total coincidence the ideal job was available.

He learned that looking for a job is a painful process and at this point in his career, it's not something he wants to do again.

If he had to do it over, he would ignore Indeed. What he received from that site was a waste of time. He strongly advises anyone to mine their network and if they don't have one, they need to build it.

He also advises everyone to be careful about burning bridges. You want to be sure to always part ways on good terms. It is a small world that is highly connected. Bottom line, your reputation and how others talk about you when you aren't in the room is all that matters.

Darren also suggests connecting with your immediate work colleagues on LinkedIn. If you suddenly get notified you are out of a job, your access to internal systems is often cut off before you get back to your desk. If all of their contact information is on your work account, you've lost those contacts.

As you get older your network is critical. If you are totally dependent on LinkedIn to find a job, you are screwed. Starting from scratch to find something new is difficult and terrifying.

The Fine Line Between Desperation and Interest

Marti is a 27-year-old writer who is transitioning into a technical writing role with her new company. She will focus on release notes, customer support articles, and customer communication. She is excited about the change.

Marti was let go from her previous job after being restructured out of her position. This was part of a larger layoff. She described the experience as heart-breaking, but believes it was for the best.

Marti's search lasted about 60 days. She knows she was very fortunate. She had anticipated six months.

When she was laid off in December 2023, she was watching massive layoffs in the tech sector. She was seeing her friends post on LinkedIn that they had been laid off and she feared the timing was terrible. Knowing this, along with having a unique degree and a limited amount of experience, she was discouraged going into the process.

Marti found it very discouraging that no one would acknowledge her application after applying for a job. She quickly realized her resume was going into an automated applicant tracking system (ATS) never to be heard from again. Marti never received rejection emails during her last search, but ironically, is getting rejection emails from jobs she applied for during her previous job search. It's like companies are clearing out their ATS system a year and a half later.

The lack of closure in so many instances made the search process hard for Marti. You just assumed no one was interested if you didn't hear back. It was also discouraging to get scheduled for an interview and have it canceled at the last minute for budget or other excuses she didn't necessarily believe.

In Marti's view, what makes the market tough is the number of people applying for fewer jobs. Marti doesn't have enough experience to lead a team. There seems to be a lot of outsourcing at the lower levels, at least in marketing. In addition, more senior-level people are getting hired to replace the people let go. The belief is they can generate more revenue than junior level staff members.

What ultimately worked for Marti was a referral from a past colleague who was working at the company that eventually hired her. She had a technical writing position and asked her to apply. Marti interviewed for the job and was told the company hired someone else with much more experience. Two weeks later, the candidate who signed the offer letter backed out. She interviewed again and didn't hear anything for two weeks. At this point she needed to be talked off the crazy ledge. She finally received a text from the recruiter on a Friday evening asking if she could talk on Monday when they offered her the job.

Marti was 250 applications deep by the time she received an offer. She continued to apply while she was interviewing. She used a niche site called Built In, which she likes better than LinkedIn.

Unlike previous times, Marti worked part-time while she was looking for a new job. She wanted to be more patient, and working part-time made that possible. Her job before the last one was not the best fit and she didn't want to make the same mistake. She believed the right opportunity would come along and wanted to avoid a panic mode.

There is a fine line between acting desperate and showing interest, and you can't show the desperate during the hiring process. Being patient has paid off. She believes she has landed in a good place. The onboarding has been so much more comprehensive, and she is already seeing the benefits.

Marti will tell you she worried too much about the optics of being let go, even though it wasn't due to performance. She had to accept it wasn't about her, and for many people, it's part of the professional experience.

She also wishes she had spent more time on her resume. That's hard to do when you don't always know where you want to end up. For Marti, getting clear about her desired destination was critical.

Marti offered these words of wisdom:

Searching For A Job Sucks!

Tap your network.

Someone knows someone who has something going on or is about to hire or someone is starting something new. It used to bother her that the world was becoming so small, and everyone knew what everyone else was doing, but now she sees the value.

Don't apply just to apply.

Be passionate and interested about the job you are applying for as opposed to shotgun applying. It doesn't work, and someone will either reject you or forget about you.

Stay organized so you can track what you apply for.

She had a spread sheet with everything she had applied for and the status of the jobs. She could see who was responding, and the data showed her where she was having her best success.

CHAPTER 3: INTERVIEW

Why You Get Hired

Job interviews haven't changed in years. While being a seriously flawed process—unstructured, full of bias, conducted by untrained and unprepared interviewers, unclear requirements—an interview is the most widely used process for evaluating candidates and making hiring decisions. We can't change the flaws, but knowing what they are and being adequately prepared is the key to success.

For starters, you would be appalled, but not entirely shocked, to know how little time and effort interviewers spend preparing for an interview. Many times, the first time they see your resume is when they walk into the interview. Sadly, the interviewer knows nothing about you or your background and must do something, so they don't appear like a complete idiot. Consequently, the interviewer does most of the talking and asks very few questions. As a result, you leave the interview wondering if they know anything about you. Afterward, the interviewer will evaluate the candidate. Based on what? That is the scary part. Interviewers make judgments about candidates when they know very little about them.

Here is another problem. Many interviews are 30 minutes long, and because many interviewers form first impressions within the first 5 minutes, it isn't enough time to evaluate a candidate fairly. I force myself to find contrary information to ensure I don't incorrectly judge someone. Unfortunately, most interviewers have never heard of contrary information and how it applies to interviewing.

The other challenge is not having clarity or shared agreement about the hiring requirements. Hiring managers don't always take the time to think through the essential hiring requirements before starting the recruiting process. What you often see is a hiring manager squeezing in a short meeting with a recruiter where they rattle off whatever they can think of at the moment before heading off to another meeting. Armed with very little information, the recruiter is expected to understand what is needed via osmosis. In addition, what you often read in a job posting is a human resources (HR) job description that may not match what the hiring manager cares about. HR job descriptions are written to satisfy the need for compliance, not for hiring. You can tell when it is filled with soft skills and statements that apply to many different jobs. For the person being interviewed, it is a challenge to know what matters most; you basically must guess.

Also, hiring managers rarely do a good job of preparing interviewing team members for their interviews. Consequently, interviewers focus on what they believe is essential, which may or may not match what matters to the hiring manager. Also, if you have multiple interviews, they are usually poorly coordinated, so you answer the same questions several times. That means some of the most important questions may never get asked.

For a job seeker to successfully navigate the interviewing process, it is essential to understand the formula some interviewers use to create interview questions. The operating assumption is that past performance is the best indicator of future performance. Personally, I can't argue with that. Therefore, behavioral interviewing is what most interviewers learn when learning how to interview. According to an article by Tomas Chamorro-Premuzic in *Forbes*: "Decades of scientific research show that the only valid or predictive job interviews are highly structured, standardized, and able to link behavioral signals to concrete indicators of future work performance. Yet when we rely on recruiters or hiring managers to pick up on these signals, our chances of success are severely limited."

As a job seeker, how often have you experienced a highly structured, standardized interview process where interviewers ask thoughtful behavioral questions? My guess is rarely. What you experience is a thrown-together, haphazard process where the criteria for making a hiring decision are vague at best.

And finally, there is the issue of bias. As much as you might like it to be otherwise, you can't eliminate people's biases. As the person being interviewed, you likely won't know what biases are in play, and you can do nothing about them. If someone is negatively predisposed toward women, Hispanics, overweight people, or people with brown eyes, there is nothing you can do to overcome that bias. Video interviewing became popular before the pandemic, and while I understand it is nice to see the person you might eventually hire, it was just another opportunity for bias to sneak into the decision-making process.

Searching For A Job Sucks!

So, What Can You Do?

Knowing all this, you may wonder how hiring managers make hiring decisions. In my years of experience, it comes down to two factors:

1. Does this person have the technical or functional skills to solve my problem?

2. Do I like this person?

Your answers to the first question are how you demonstrate your technical and functional skills to the interviewer. Now is the time to provide examples of your expertise and accomplishments. If you share your experiences this way, it doesn't take long for someone to determine if you have the right technical or functional background. You can't fake this. You have it or you don't.

Once you answer the first question, it all comes down to the second question: Do they like you? Whether you call it "fit," "chemistry," or "personal connection," it is all the same. The subconscious kicks in, and hiring managers find themselves attracted to some candidates more than others. Don't ask me to explain why; it's just how the process works and how we are wired as humans. The intangible is hard to measure and very subjective to assess. As a job seeker, this is somewhat out of your control but not entirely.

One aspect of the interview you can control that can make a huge difference is to relax and be yourself. That means being comfortable with who you are, confident in your ability, and clear about what you offer. Don't press, and don't appear anxious or desperate. Relax, take a deep breath, and smile. The more you let go of what you can't control, the better you will do.

I often tell people to think of this meeting as something other than an interview. Think of it as a conversation between people with like-minded interests. Remove the hierarchy in your mind. Aside from demonstrating what you know technically and functionally, your objective is to decide if you like the people you are meeting. Do you want to spend 8 to 10 hours a day with them? Do you sense a connection or chemistry? Do they care about the same things you care about?

Remember, this is a two-way street. You have lots of choices in this matter. While you want to show genuine interest, it is vital to assess what you can about the culture, the people, and how they work. It is also okay to ask for more time or another meeting to make this assessment if you need more data to make a good decision. One or two interviews aren't always enough time to know if this is the right choice. Ask for an opportunity to shadow someone for half a day to see what the day-to-day is like.

You can't be someone you aren't. If you don't feel it, the interviewer probably didn't feel it either. This is where bias, good or bad, leaks into the hiring process. It's why you rarely, if ever, get feedback when you interview. Hiring decisions are often hard to explain, and sometimes, to justify. That is why you need to relax and enjoy the experience for what it is—a chance to meet some interesting people who care about the same things you do and the opportunity to extend your network.

Interviewing isn't easy for many, but this is especially true for people who do it very infrequently. How can you tip the outcome of an interview in your favor? To keep it simple, think about the interview in three parts:

Searching For A Job Sucks!

- Before the interview
- During the interview
- After the interview

As you review this outline, you will notice quickly that more time is spent before the interview than anywhere else. That's not an accident. The absolute key to a successful interview will coincide with the time you spend preparing.

Before the Interview

Know Your Audience

Do adequate research and learn as much as possible about the company, its products and services, key competitors, culture, industry challenges, and the people you will meet. If the company is publicly traded, listen to the last earnings call for insight into what's important. Read the company's website to understand what it does and what products and services it offers. Find its competitors and look for challenges. You will likely be able to read about the culture on the website.

You may also find current news about the organization. If possible, use LinkedIn to find people who have left the organization. Send them a connection request and see if they will engage in a conversation.

You can even try asking ChatGPT to give you a list of the top challenges a particular company is facing. Or the top five challenges someone in a particular role might face. Knowing this, you can prepare answers to related questions or offer input using the formula discussed further on in this chapter.

Know the Job

Review the job description to understand the top requirements. While the soft stuff matters, focus on the technical and functional skills required to be successful. Your expertise, whatever that might be, is why they have chosen to speak with you. Understand your technical abilities and functional skills thoroughly and link them directly to the job's specific requirements. This alignment will demonstrate how your expertise matches the needs of the role.

Remember, a job description doesn't always capture the requirements that matter most to a hiring manager. Talk to the people who have held similar roles to understand what really matters. This deeper dive into the role will help you develop the stories you need to demonstrate your qualifications.

Prepare Your Narrative

Your preparation will fall into three categories:

1. Stories

2. Questions you can ask to create a great conversation

3. Answers to questions you might get asked

You prepare and practice stories in advance to demonstrate your skills, experience, and fit.

Searching For A Job Sucks!

Your stories will focus on how you have used your technical and functional skills to solve problems or tackle opportunities. If hiring managers ask behavioral interviewing questions, you want to prepare examples that will answer them. If they don't ask behavioral interviewing questions, this is a great way to give them the information they need to assess your capability.

A way to formulate those answers is with the acronym SAR:

Situation: What challenge, opportunity, problem, and so on did you face? Be specific about the circumstances. Offer a situation that aligns with what you believe the interviewer cares about.

Action: What did you do or say to get results? Adjectives that speak to planning, doing, executing, and so on, while striking a balance between I and we, will be important. You can't solve big problems or tackle huge challenges alone; it takes a team.

Result: What was the outcome, deliverable, or result, and why did it matter? Quantify your example as much as possible. If you have chosen something the interviewer cares about, they will be very interested.

So, what was the situation you were facing? What action did you take? What was the result?

These can be short, 90-second stories that can pack a powerful punch.

Your examples are where you weave in what you know to be critical about the culture. If teamwork matters, weave in being a team player as part of your example. If good interpersonal skills matter, weave in how you applied your interpersonal skills to achieve the desired outcome. Rather than telling someone you are a team player and have good interpersonal skills, use an example where the interviewer can see those skills in action.

Remember, most interviewers are poorly prepared. As you get a sense of what's important during the interview, you want to artfully interject and say, "May I give you an example of how I have handled a situation like that in the past?" or "I hear your concern or interest in XYZ, can I tell you about a time when I dealt with something very similar" or "That sounds very much like a problem we dealt with previously, can I tell you about it?" By preparing your stories in advance, you can pull on the ones you need based on what the interviewer might find most interesting. The hidden value of this approach is that it takes the interviewer off the hook and makes them more comfortable.

Another aspect of preparation concerns questions you can ask. Use your research about the industry, the company, and the culture to generate questions that help you get smarter about the opportunity and demonstrate your preparation and interest in the role. Remember, you are interviewing them as much as they are interviewing you. As much as possible, tailor the questions to your interviewer:

- Why is the position open?

- What are the most significant challenges facing this department or organization?

- What must this role accomplish in the first 6 to 12 months?

Searching For A Job Sucks!

- What will be critical to the organization's success in the future?

- Describe how the various teams/departments work together inside the organization.

- How does conflict get resolved?

- If the role requires you to manage people, how are the best leaders successful?

There is a hidden reason behind asking the questions like the preceding ones. The answers provide an opportunity to use your stories to tell the interviewer how you addressed a similar problem or opportunity in the past. Thoughtful questions allow you to demonstrate your capability to the interviewer. You must usually lead your interviewer to these questions and answers. At the end of an interview, you'll have time to ask questions about why people have left in the past, how people get onboarded, or the timeline for deciding.

Believe it or not, most interviewers don't understand the one question that can completely change the direction of an interview. Knowing this gives you a significant advantage over other candidates. You aim to turn the interview into a conversation and have the interviewer listen intently to every word you say. Asking questions and probing deeper will help convince the interviewer that you are absolutely the perfect candidate.

This same question applies to almost any job and at any organizational level. You may be a great cultural fit, but if this one question goes unanswered or is answered poorly.

Again, the question is simply this: *Can you solve my problem?*

Ultimately, this is what every interview is all about. A job opening represents an opportunity to solve problems or tackle new challenges. The size of the problem or challenge may be large or small, depending on the role or the opportunity, but the answer to this question is at the core of what every hiring manager tries to determine.

Here is your challenge as a candidate: you can't assume the interviewer understands the importance of this question or even knows how to ask it. The candidate needs to tee this up to ensure the necessary conversation takes place.

The best way to do this during an interview is to ask a question as clearly and concisely as possible: *Why is this job important? What needs to be accomplished that isn't happening now?*

How can this job impact the business?

If the issue or opportunity is unclear or lacks adequate context, ask a clarifying question before diving in with your answer. Having the hiring manager talk more about their challenge provides an opportunity to empathize with what they are facing, which helps to build a connection. It is also a great way to learn more about the issue. You want your answer to be totally on target.

With this clear understanding, you can pull on your stories and examples to steer the conversation. Whether the interviewer understands this, you are now talking about what matters. You are talking about actual pain points and problems or opportunities that need to be solved.

Searching For A Job Sucks!

Your research before an interview is critical. Knowing the answer to your question in advance puts you in a great position to demonstrate insight and thoughtfulness. You want the hiring manager to see you in the role tomorrow. You want to be seen as the answer to all their problems. If you can accomplish that during an interview, you significantly increase your chance of getting an offer.

The third aspect of preparation deals with what you will be asked during the interview. Whether in front of a mirror or front of friends or loved ones, practice your answers and know what it feels like when you are smiling. Listen to your voice to ensure there is adequate enthusiasm. Keep your hands on the table, palms up, or in a steeple position. Don't act like you are conducting an orchestra. Here are possible questions you might encounter:

- Why are we talking?
- Tell me about yourself.
- What is your greatest accomplishment in your last role?
- What is your greatest strength?
- What is your greatest weakness?
- Describe your contribution as part of a successful project.
- Why are you interested?
- What do you like to do when you are not working?
- Why did you leave your last position?

- How would others describe your leadership style?

- Why are you pursuing a role for which you may seem overqualified?

- Why is there a gap in your employment?

- Why are you looking?

- Where would you like to be five years from now?

While there are many other questions you may be asked, preparing for these will be a good start. Ask a close friend or mentor to listen to your answers before an interview so you are clear, concise, and convincing.

Anticipate

You know your work history better than anyone, so prepare for those questions you can likely anticipate. For example, be able to explain the following:

- Gaps in employment

- Short tenure

- Why you are looking

- Why you are pursuing a role for which you may seem overqualified

While these may be uncomfortable topics, it's essential to be honest. Take responsibility for your decisions, and if you've made a mistake in the past, say so. It happens. It's part of the learning process.

Searching For A Job Sucks!

Regardless of the answer, it's crucial for the interviewer to hear your commitment to working hard and desire to contribute.

Practice

Practice your responses so you can see and hear yourself answering questions. Like any competitive athlete, the more repetitions the better. Pay attention to your body language and tone of voice. I often tell people to smile as a way to demonstrate confidence and to connect with the interviewer. Stand in front of a mirror and see what you look and sound like answering questions. If you don't like what you see, make some adjustments now while you still can.

LinkedIn offers a free AI-powered Interview Prep Tool (https://www.linkedIn.com/interview-prep). It is easy to use, and your AI coach will give you feedback on how you answered. You can even ask close connections to give you feedback.

Money

While it may or may not come up, preparing yourself to talk about money is essential.

Following the guidance discussed earlier in the book, if asked what you expect, you don't want to give a definitive answer before knowing everything you can about the role, how you can contribute, and all of the components associated with compensation. Compensation is more than base salary—it also includes bonus, potential sign-on, benefits, vacation, 401(k), and so on.

You never want to sell yourself short and ask for too little, but you also don't want to ask for so much that the request seems ridiculous.

The best strategy is to use third-party research or what you know about the industry, and tell the person asking what a job like this should pay, not necessarily what you want or expect. Don't set an expectation until you have more data.

Don't think of yourself as a candidate; think of yourself as a solution that will help the organization accomplish strategic goals and solve complex problems. Eventually, you'll need to ask for and potentially negotiate the compensation package you believe you deserve.

Know Your Numbers

As an executive or manager, you'll be expected to know the details associated with your operation. Having details around cost, quality, delivery, customer satisfaction, and employee engagement at your fingertips will be essential. You'll likely be asked to explain the actions that led to the results you have achieved.

Research the People You Will Meet

Find out everything you can about the people who will be interviewing you. LinkedIn and the company website can provide valuable information about the individuals you will meet. It's okay to ask for an agenda in advance of the interview so you know who will be part of the process. You may find common interests, backgrounds, schools, and so on, making personal connections easier

Logistics

You will want to confirm the interview's date, time, location, and format (in-person, video, panel, and so on). Arrive 10 to 15 minutes early, but not any earlier. It's awkward for everyone if you arrive too early. Make sure you have the interviewer's contact information in case of emergencies or unexpected delays.

If this is a video call, test in advance that the technology is working.

Dress

Unless instructed otherwise, my advice is to always wear formal business attire. It is always better to be overdressed than underdressed. It goes without saying that you need to look your best —neat, clean, and well-groomed.

During the Interview

It all begins when the interviewer extends their hand and says, "Hello." Shake hands firmly, make eye contact, and smile. What happens in the next 30 to 60 minutes can determine whether you are successful and receive an offer. While much of this is outside your control, the following suggestions can increase your chances of success.

It's critical to stay in the moment and not get ahead of yourself. This may sound odd, but your objective isn't to get a job; your objective is to get to the next step in the process. Focus on the task at hand and don't get ahead of yourself. Even if you think the interviewing process is all for show and nothing more than a check-a-box exercise, you want to focus on how you can crush the current interview and don't worry about what comes next. Every interaction with a recruiter or anyone from the hiring organization is an interview, and don't forget that.

Success starts with making an excellent first impression. Dress professionally, arrive 15 minutes early, be friendly with everyone, smile, look the interviewer(s) in the eye, and with a firm handshake, say "Hello."

After that, you have one crucial objective—which you may find very surprising. While getting an offer is obvious, the more important objective at this very moment, is to make the interviewer feel comfortable! That's right. You may think a successful interview is about your background, experience, and ability to answer questions. Of course, that matters, but it's not enough. Your success in the interview often has more to do with your ability to connect with your interviewer. There are several ways you can make that happen.

Mirror

Quickly pick up the interviewer's affect and begin to mirror that back. This is a great way to build rapport and make the interviewer feel comfortable. In an updated May 22, 2013, *Forbes* article titled "Want to Nail an Interview? Use Mirroring," *mirroring* is defined as "the practice of adopting another person's behaviors, mannerisms, and ways of speaking. When performed well, it's as if you become a mirror image of the other person." I don't mean to suggest that you copy or mimic the other person. It is more subtle. You need to be somewhat upbeat and energetic if they are upbeat and energetic. You need to be quiet and reserved if they are quiet and reserved. If someone is serious-minded and all business, you need to be serious-minded and all business. If they use specific language or terms, use the same language. People feel most comfortable with people who are like themselves, and using mirroring makes it easier to build rapport and create a connection. On the other hand, if someone seems disinterested or annoyed, you still need to be positive and friendly, just not over the top.

Ask Questions

As previously stated, interviewers are often unprepared and need help figuring out what to ask. By using questions you prepared in advance, you can turn this interview into a conversation, which is much more comfortable for most interviewers. When you ask questions, it gives you an opportunity to go deep and to demonstrate your expertise on a particular topic. Use what you hear as a launching point to discuss other topics you know the interviewer will find interesting and helpful. Asking thoughtful questions creates a different dynamic. It is now two colleagues talking about a topic they both find interesting. Don't think about it as an interview. Think about it as a conversation with two like-minded individuals who share a common interest. Asking questions allows you to listen like someone who wants to help, not impress. Think about the interview as a way to build a relationship and not a step in the job-seeking process. Approaching an interview with this frame of mind can remove whatever pressure you may be feeling and make the experience more enjoyable.

Listen

Actively listen carefully by nodding your head and rephrasing what the interviewer says. You want the interviewer to feel heard and respected. They will often interpret your understanding as shared interest and or agreement. It may not be, but that's what you want them to think for now

Examples

When interviewers are uncomfortable, they tend to do all the talking. The SAR formula—Situation, Action, and Result—reviewed earlier changes the dynamic. It allows the unprepared interviewer to do more listening and puts the focus on you, where it belongs. The more you get to share, the more accurately the interviewer can assess your background and will make them sound brilliant in a wrap-up meeting.

Affirmation

As the interviewer discusses important points, acknowledge their perspective and how it aligns with your own experience and beliefs. Finding points where you can establish agreement makes it easier to connect. You can decide afterward if you truly agree with what they are saying.

Professionalism

Don't get so relaxed that you make a careless comment or act too chummy. This can make an interviewer uncomfortable. Maintain good eye contact and smile at appropriate moments. Don't say anything negative about your previous employer. Stay positive with an eye toward the future.

Interest

Tell them you appreciated their time and enjoyed meeting and hearing their insight and perspective. You want them to believe they did a great job as an interviewer—even if they were terrible. Be sure to tell them how interested you are in the opportunity and the chance to work together. Once you have an offer, you can ask more challenging questions, assess your fit, and decide if it's the right opportunity. That will never happen unless you establish a good connection with the interviewer by helping them feel more comfortable.

Connection with the Culture

One of your goals during the interviewing process is to connect with the culture. While every organization will tell you its culture is unique, most look for three aspects during the interview.

The first is interpersonal and relationship skills. How well did you connect with the interviewer? Were you friendly? Are you a good listener? Do you get along well with others?

The second is teamwork and collaboration. Did you come across as someone who plays well with others? Did you focus on "me" versus "we"? How did you help others succeed? How did you share? How did you make those around you successful? Did you treat everyone you met—from the receptionist to the most senior-level executive—with the utmost respect?

The third is enthusiasm. Did you come across as interested in the role and the company? Can I hear the enthusiasm in your voice? Did I hear passion and excitement about the opportunity? Is there a smile on your face and excitement in your eyes?

Panel Interviews

A panel interview is often part of the interviewing process. For starters, it saves the company time. With everyone seeing you at once, interviewers can compare notes and quickly decide. It also gives the interviewers an opportunity to see how you interact with the team and determine the degree of fit.

From a candidate's perspective, panel interviews can be very challenging. How do you stand out? How do you keep as many as five or six people interested in what you have to say? How do you address everyone so no one feels ignored? How do you handle the rapid fire of questions both clearly and concisely?

Get to know your interviewers in advance

It is all right to ask who will be on the panel in advance of your interview. You will want to research each interviewer, so they seem less like strangers when you walk into the room. Learn their names, what they have in common, what makes them important to the process, and what they might care about. Knowing this information will make it easier to establish a personal connection. This will also help you prepare questions that focus on each person's skill and expertise.

Introduce Yourself to Each Interviewer

Go up to each person to introduce yourself. Offer a firm handshake and a smile and let them know you are happy to meet them. Meeting everyone like this may seem awkward, but a quick "Hi, everyone" doesn't make the best first impression. If you repeat their name aloud, after they tell it to you, it might help you remember. As much as possible, place your attention on connecting with each individual on a professional level.

Jot Down Names

One trick is to quickly jot down everyone's name in the order in which they are seated. You can now include the person's name when you answer their question.

Address the Person Asking the Question

You can only answer one question at a time. Address your answer to the person asking the question while making eye contact with the rest of the panel. A panel seems much more manageable when you aren't trying to address everyone simultaneously. Take extra copies of your resume.

Don't assume everyone has read or even seen your resume. Take extra copies and let the panel know you have additional copies if anyone needs to see one.

Don't Fill the Dead Spots

During a panel interview, there will often be moments of silence as the interviewers decide who will go next. Don't rush in to fill the void. Just sit quietly and wait for the next question.

Identify the Key Decision-Maker

All panel members are not created equal. Identify the key decision maker. You'll want to make eye contact with this person more often than the other panel members. You don't want to ignore the others, but this is the person you'll most want to impress. More frequently than not, this person will be the hiring manager.

Do Your Homework

You can't hide during a panel interview. It is more critical than ever that you have done your homework and know as much as you can about the industry, the culture, the problems, and opportunities the organization is facing, and where it is headed. This puts you in a better position to not only answer questions but also ask questions. The more you can turn this into a conversation, the better.

Panel interviews can seem intimidating, but they can be easily managed with the right amount of preparation. Just stay in the moment and remember that you can only answer one question at a time.

Video Calls

When you talk about interviewing, you need to talk about the emergence of video calls. For example, many initial screens have gone from phone calls to video calls using Zoom. While you need to prepare for a video call the same way you do for any interview, some differences are worth noting. Here are some tips for making the best impression:

- Find a quiet location and shut out distractions. You don't want the dog barking or children screaming in the background. Never ask the interviewer to hold while you answer a call or respond to a text message. Trust me, it happens.

Searching For A Job Sucks!

- Make sure the technology is working in advance. Log in five minutes before the call to ensure your audio and video work. If you use a cell phone, ensure you have good reception. You don't want the call to drop mid-interview.

- Develop a cheat sheet and have it discreetly in front of you during the interview. Are there data points about the organization you want to remember? Are there particular skills you want to highlight? Are there specific accomplishments you want to share?

- Have a copy of your resume in front of you and be in a position where you can take notes.

- Shower, groom, and dress as if you are meeting someone face to face. Looking professional makes you feel more professional. You want to communicate confidence and energy but you can't do that in your pajamas. And, like it or not, appearance matters. Why do you think they started using video calls for interviews in the first place?

- Watch your posture. Sit up straight, and don't slouch. Don't lie in bed and expect to make a positive impression. People often project better when they are standing up.

- Have your camera at eye level. No one wants to look up your nose. Also, look at the camera, not the screen. Keep your background neutral and professional.

- Be sure to smile while speaking to convey positive body language and confidence. The tone of your voice will matter. Have a glass of water handy. You can practice this in advance in front of a mirror.

Closing

Before leaving, thank the interviewer for their time and express your interest in the opportunity. Ask about the next steps and when you can expect to hear something.

After the Interview

Send Thank-You Notes

If you have ever wondered about the importance of writing a thank-you note after an interview, it matters. I have clients who take special notice when a candidate fails to follow up.

A well-written, grammatically correct, and thoughtful thank-you note in an email may be the difference in getting an offer or another interview. Long after you have left the premises, this is your way of leaving a lasting, positive impression.

While the content of your thank-you letter matters, it is the thought and even the effort that counts. Writing a personalized note to each reader communicates how much you appreciate their time and how much this opportunity matters to you. Comment on something they shared or a question they asked.

Whether you meet with three, six, or even nine people, they should all receive a note. The notes may follow the same format, but as just stated, they should capture something unique to each conversation. Thank you notes need to be short and to the point.

Searching For A Job Sucks!

And, yes, it is acceptable to send these messages via e-mail. Promptness matters in this digital age, so the sooner you get back to people, the better.

Here is a format you may find helpful.

Dear Mr./Ms. XXX,

Thank you for meeting with me today to discuss the XYZ position. I enjoyed our conversation, and I am very excited about the possibility of joining your team.

I listened to you describe the challenges and opportunities associated with this role, I believe I am a very good fit:

1. *Example one*

2. *Example two*

3. *Example three*

4. *Example four*

As someone who enjoys building relationships and being part of a team, I will enjoy being part of the XYZ culture.

Again, thank you for meeting with me and considering me for this exciting opportunity. I look forward to hearing from you.

Best regards,

This is a general format to follow. In the first paragraph, you say thank you and express your interest. You want people to know how much you appreciate their time, consideration, and willingness to meet with you. The second paragraph is where you reinforce what makes you a great candidate. The third paragraph is where you comment on your fit with the culture. In the fourth paragraph, you restate your interest and keen desire to hear back.

When you highlight your accomplishments, consider what you heard during your interviews and what problems must be solved. Present accomplishments that reinforce the immediate value you can bring to the organization.

Thank-you notes can also address additional strengths and accomplishments that didn't come up during the interview. The more you can quantify your examples, the better. All of this may help you move to the next step in the process.

Finally, make sure you proofread your letter carefully. Typos and grammatical errors are unprofessional and sloppy and can cost you the job. Trust me, I've seen that happen often.

If you don't hear anything in the expected timeframe, it's okay to check in on the status of the process. Hopefully you will hear back. You will appear desperate if you circle back more than once a week after you expected to hear. It's also possible you will never hear anything back, but don't take it personally. Just recognize that's the level of rudeness and lack of respect you can expect if you ever go to work for that company.

Review and Reflect

Do a post-mortem on the entire experience. What would you start doing? What would you stop doing? What would you continue doing? Use what you learn or relearn so you can perform better the next time you read for a part.

Let Go of the Outcome

At this point, you've done almost all you can. Now, you have to wait, be patient, and follow up after a reasonable amount of time (I recommend five business days after your last interview). After that, give it another week. If you don't hear something right away, it doesn't always mean bad news. This process never goes as fast as you would like.

It's also important to remember, that regardless of how anxious or even desperate you might feel, you have a choice. Be honest with yourself and if this isn't right, politely say so and excuse yourself from the process. Knowingly taking the wrong job will only land you back into job seeker mode. You want to be excited about the opportunity so you will perform your best. It's tough to be a top performer when you aren't excited about the work.

Key Messages

Knowing that most interviewers are unprepared and potentially untrained, your preparation is critical for a successful outcome. When you are adequately prepared and have good examples and questions, you can turn the interview into a conversation. This is how you establish a personal connection and convince the interviewer you are someone they like and someone they would enjoy working with. While it's important to have good answers to tough questions, it's not enough if you expect an offer.

CHAPTER 3: INTERVIEW - Why You Get Hired

Most of us are not professional interviewees. Part of preparation needs to be actual practice with a close friend or family member and even in front of mirror. Pay attention to how you share examples, your hands, your face, and your level of interest and enthusiasm. Most of all, smile!

Coaching Questions

- What makes interviewing difficult and what can you do differently?

- How can you be better prepared?

- What can you do to present yourself better?

Searching For A Job Sucks!

What's Below the Waterline?

Recruiters and hiring managers love to talk about their culture. At one point or another, we've all heard the same lines—collaborative, team-oriented, family-friendly, diverse, fun, social, opportunities for advancement, flexibility, a family, and so on.

You walk away in love with what you've heard and think "What a fantastic opportunity." Until you join and find out it isn't, and then it is too late.

As a job seeker, you need to understand something about culture—most executives don't have a clue about their actual culture. And if they do, they sure won't tell you the truth if they are trying to hire you. An executive might believe in the importance of culture and even craft an aspirational statement about their culture. However, those statements don't always reflect reality, and most of these statements are written for one of several reasons:

- HR shamed them into writing a culture statement.

- HR or Communications wrote the statement for them.

- In the one class they took on organizational behavior, the executive learned that culture is important, so you better write a culture statement.

I know this is a broad generalization, but in my experience, most executives care more about the appearance of culture than what actually exists. What they say about their organization makes it true in their mind and to the people listening. In truth, most executives live in a sheltered world, focused on economic and financial macro decisions, far from the day-to-day where the actual culture is happening in the real world. To truly understand culture, watch what happens on the ground floor where work gets done.

For example, how often have you heard executives discuss their organization as a family? That's fine until the company needs to lay off some percentage of the workforce to meet financial targets. Would you ever lay off family members and un-invite them to Thanksgiving dinner? Talk about awkward.

Here is the other reality about culture. You can tell what an executive team cares most about by looking at how they behave. What behaviors do they reward that seem counter to the stated culture? What do the policies they approve say about their deeply held beliefs and values? What do their choices tell us when they have difficult decisions to make? Where do they spend money and make investments? Who gets promoted into leadership? A company's culture reflects what a leadership team values—not necessarily what you see on the website. What the leadership team values is the culture that trickles down through the organization.

Never forget that for-profit organizations exist for one reason: to make money, and if they are publicly traded, to satisfy their shareholders. That isn't a criticism; it's a fact. It is also the case that making money excuses behavior contrary to the stated culture.

Some executives may vehemently disagree with what I'm saying. I'm sure there are exceptions, and if you look hard enough, maybe you'll find them. And if I am wrong, so what! My advice is the same: don't believe everything you hear and look for evidence of the contrary.

Searching For A Job Sucks!

So, What Can You Do?

Unfortunately, statements about culture aren't all that helpful or informative. What's essential for you as a job seeker is uncovering the truth. You are on a mission to discover disconfirming information.

There is a very well-understood reality about culture that most organizations would prefer you not think about. Culture is like an iceberg. What you can see above the waterline represents what people tell you and what you read on the website. We also know icebergs are deceptive because two-thirds of an iceberg are below the waterline, and that's the danger. While hitting an iceberg may not be as catastrophic to your career as it was for the *Titanic*, it can be enormously painful and derailing. As a job seeker, you want to do a better job than the *Titanic* and avoid those hidden dangers. As a candidate, focus more on what's below the waterline to avoid making a wrong choice.

In a *Forbes* article titled "5 Marks of a Toxic Work Culture—And How You Know It's Time to Leave," Mark C. Perna provided a helpful list from ClearForce CEO Tom Miller of what you find in a toxic environment:

- Bullying
- Harassment
- Unethical practices
- Dishonesty

- Low pay

- Exceptional performance goes unrewarded

- Prioritizes customers over employees

- Limits internal mobility

- Employees don't feel safe, supported or heard

- Requires employees to be on call 24/7

In an article by Donald Sull, Charles Sull, and Ben Zweig, published by *MIT Sloan Management Review* titled "Toxic Culture Is Driving the Great Resignation," work culture was noted as the No. 1 reason people cited for leaving their jobs. Organic marketing platform Conductor analyzed Google search volume in 2022 and found that searches for "toxic work environment quiz" increased 700% in April alone. The conductor also found that "HIPAA violations in the workplace" searches increased by 350%, "workplace mobbing" searches increased by 190%, and "top workplaces 2022" searches increased by 500%."

So then, how does a job seeker see through the BS when hiring managers, executives, and most certainly human resources (HR) talk about culture? This responsibility falls on the job seeker to understand what lies beneath the waterline.

Before ever agreeing to an interview, doing your research is critical. You need firsthand testimonials from people you can trust to be honest. That is harder than you think because people are often uncomfortable sharing anything that might come back to bite them.

Searching For A Job Sucks!

They are also reluctant to share anything that might not be popular or that might overly influence your decision. You must assure them that you want the unvarnished truth and that whatever you decide is your responsibility. Once you are fully informed, you can choose how best to proceed or not.

The LinkedIn database of names can help with this research. Find people who have recently left the organization, even ones doing similar work, and ask if you can have a confidential conversation. I'm less inclined to rely on sources like Glassdoor because those who spend time pontificating on Glassdoor are often unhappy and have an axe to grind. I'm looking for people to discuss what's above and below the waterline. You need a balanced perspective to make a good decision. It may be that you have a friend who has a friend who recently left the organization. That is the person you want to reach.

I have generated a list of questions, in no particular order, that can help identify what lies beneath the waterline. These questions can be used in your data gathering before an interview. The same questions can also be used during the interviewing process and after you receive an offer to understand the reality of what you'll be facing. Choose the questions that seem most important, given the organization.

While the answers to these questions will be helpful, how people react can be even more illuminating. You don't have to be a trained psychologist to read body language. Do people hesitate, do they answer the question, do they ramble? Do they seem uncomfortable? Are they enthusiastic? Remember, this is a two-way street, and you are on a reconnaissance mission. Pay attention to everything you see and hear.

Before you ever say "yes," it's imperative to understand the reality of what you will be facing. Don't underestimate the importance of culture. You not only want to succeed in a new role, but you also want to be happy.

What do you like about working here?

What you hear aligns with your values and how you like to work. Do you hear anything that isn't a good fit? Ask everyone you meet and listen for common themes.

When people leave the organization voluntarily, what are the reasons they leave?

If people tell you they don't know, I hear alarm bells. You don't think people talk about this? You can also ask if the organization has any data they can share.

What are the learning and development opportunities that employees take advantage of?

Having a long list of training and development opportunities is one thing. Getting permission and the time to participate is quite different. How much of the cost is covered?

What do you wish someone told you before joining the organization?

If they quickly answer, it's something they have thought about. No organization is perfect, so you should expect to hear something.

Searching For A Job Sucks!

What would you change if you had a magic wand and could change anything about the organization's culture?

Listen for themes in what you hear. I'd be worried if someone doesn't know or isn't saying.

How do leaders respond when expectations aren't met?

Ask if the leadership comes forward to take responsibility. Ask for an example that shows character and integrity. Does the organization engage in blaming?

If you do an employee satisfaction survey, what is the greatest concern expressed by employees?

How does this concern tie back to organizational values?

What are the behaviors that tend to get rewarded and recognized here?

Listen for behaviors that align with your values and emulate how you operate

How does the organization support mental and physical well-being?

Does the organization provide flexibility when needed? Does it trust its employees to get their work accomplished? Are there policies and programs in place that encourage balance? Are resources and accommodations available for people working from home

Based on who gets promoted, what does it take to advance in this organization? Listen here for the behaviors that matter if you want to succeed.

Looking back, what would you tell yourself if you had the opportunity to give yourself advice as a new hire?

What you hear is valuable and critical to success. Pay attention!

You obviously can't ask one person all of these questions but ask each interviewer 2 or 3. When you have the opportunity, ask a question to more than one person. You'll also want to ask a question to multiple people if an answer raises a serious red flag.

Another way to assess an organization's culture that often gets overlooked is to pay close attention to your experience as a candidate. I've learned this from working with many organizations and watching how they manage the recruiting, interviewing, and hiring process.

Here is what you can expect from an organization with a well-developed recruiting, interviewing, and hiring process:

- They have a well-defined and articulated hiring process.

- The requirements for the role they are trying to fill are clear and precise, and you know what is required to succeed.

- After each interview, you hear back within three to five days.

- People return your calls when you have questions.

Searching For A Job Sucks!

- Interviewers have read your resume before the interview and have questions prepared in advance.

- If they make an offer, how well does it align with your expectations? There are no huge surprises.

- The process moves along crisply.

- There are no more than three to five interviews.

- They can decide without lots of delay and endless layers of approval.

- Interviewers answer your questions honestly.

Here is what you can expect from an organization with a weak recruiting, interviewing, and hiring process:

- The requirements for the role aren't precise and seem to shift.

- It takes weeks to hear back after you interview.

- Your calls are not always returned.

- People show up for your interviews late and unprepared.

- The interviewing process seems disorganized.

- You have more than three to five interviews.

- There are multiple people in each interview.

- It takes forever for the organization to make a decision

- The offer is below market.

I point this out for one reason that is worth noting: what you experience as a candidate is what you will experience as an employee. I have seen this play out over and over so there is no reason to be surprised.

Finally, there is one last red flag about the culture that is important for you to understand. If someone in HR or one of your interviewers says they are working to change the culture—be very careful. It might be time to run away as fast as you can. Changing the culture is code for things being a mess.

Unless you are hired to be the CEO or a very senior leader, there is very little you can do to change culture. There are experts on the topic such as the late Edgar Schein from MIT who believed you can't change culture. And even if it does change slightly, it will take years to become the organization people aspire to. Is this something you want to sign up for?

Key Messages

The notion of what's below the waterline is critical to understand and embrace. I've seen smart, talented people go into organizations and either fail, be unhappy or both. It's not like someone takes the "stupid" pill before they start a new job. Something else is causing the disconnect and its often a culture different from what they expected.

Many times, there were warning signals during the interviewing process that were ignored, either because of their desire to make a change, or because of the favorable attention and affirmation they received. When you are being courted, it's easy to get carried away in the moment and ignore what your gut is trying to tell you. It's not like someone takes the "stupid" pill before they start a new job. Something else has changed and its often a different reality of the culture.

View the interviewing process as a reconnaissance mission. Go beyond what people tell you about the culture and find other resources to do your own due diligence. If you decide to say yes to an offer, go in with your eyes wide open knowing there is probably nothing you can change about the existing culture. You want to be sure you can you live with the tradeoffs.

One of your best data points about culture is your experience as a candidate. Pay close attention to what you experience as a candidate. It is likely what you will experience as an employee.

Coaching Questions

- What questions have you missed in the past that you want to ask in the future?

- What other resources or people can help you get a realistic preview of the culture?

- What is your gut telling you?

CHAPTER 3: INTERVIEW - Why You Get Hired

HR Can Only Say "No"

Very often your first interview after passing the recruiter screen, is with HR. HR typically plays two roles. The first is to welcome you. They like to tell you about the company, the culture, the benefits. They typically can't ask you questions about the technical or functional requirements of a job because they don't know what they are.

The second role is to determine if a candidate would be a good cultural fit. It must be written on a tablet some place that the best person to assess cultural fit or leadership potential is HR. The irony here is that HR lives in the land of aspiration and make believe, and thinks the actual culture is what they read on the website. Sorry Tinker Bell, that isn't the case. Furthermore, most HR people have lived their entire professional life in staff roles and have never had operating responsibility.

In either scenario, as my friend and colleague Andy likes to say, while HR can't say "yes," they can say "no." HR can't make the decision to hire someone, but they can submarine a good candidate for all the wrong reasons. That's why the HR interview is important. If HR determines you wouldn't be a good "fit," it is hard to recover. Hiring managers, out of fear, lack of confidence, internal process, or for some unknown reason, often defer to HR to make this judgment. It is important to remember that HR isn't your friend in this process. It views itself as guardian of the galaxy and continually tries to justify its existence by exerting power wherever it sees the opportunity. Sometimes that means saying "no" just because they can.

Searching For A Job Sucks!

Shari Caudron wrote a 2002 article for workforce.com that captures the way job seekers feel about HR and this echoes what I have heard for years. "Talk to jobseekers today—especially in heavily downsized industries such as high-tech and telecommunications—and you'll discover they are so fed up with the perceived arrogance, disrespect, and ineffectiveness of HR that they are doing everything they can to avoid the function altogether."

I'm sure you are saying to yourself, "This article was written a long time ago; I'm sure things have changed." Nope. Nomore Mbombera wrote "41 Reasons Why Job Seekers Hate HR Professionals" in 2024. After reading both of these articles, you have to ask yourself why we even need HR, but that's two-beer discussion for another time.

How ironic that the function charged with winning the so called "war on talent" is viewed by applicants as an obstacle to success.

So, What Can You Do?

You can start by preparing examples that demonstrate your use of soft skills, or what many consider as people skills. What are the traits this company hires for? In a *Forbes* article titled "11 Essential Soft Skills in 2024 (With Examples)," Monique Danao listed the following:

- Communication
- Leadership
- Teamwork
- Creativity

CHAPTER 3: INTERVIEW - Why You Get Hired

- Time Management
- Adaptability
- Problem Solving
- Work Ethic
- Critical Thinking
- Conflict Management
- Emotional Intelligence

It is a very good bet that HR will be looking to ask you questions about one or more of these areas depending on the role. While your technical and functional skills represent absolute "musts" for getting hired, it is your soft skills that will differentiate you from the other candidates. This is why you need to play nice with HR. Others will look to HR to provide an evaluation of your soft skills.

Knowing that about HR, there are several keys to acing the HR interview and working with HR that are worth passing along.

- First and foremost, act interested and excited about the opportunity to meet with HR. HR likes to feel valued and respected, so you need to show this deference during the interview. This is probably a statement of the obvious, but you'd be surprised by how many candidates look past this interview and don't get another opportunity.

- Do enough homework about the company, the products, and the culture so you can ask one or two intelligent questions. Just because someone is in HR doesn't mean they know how to interview people. Thoughtful questions turn the interview into a conversation and that often leads to a connection with HR.

- When answering questions, blend in behaviors that align with their stated culture. For example, "When we accomplished XYZ project and I had to build a closely knit team with IT and Finance to ensure a successful integration." This is how you demonstrate the soft skills that HR wants to hear.

- Be pleasant and friendly. You want to make a good impression so if this opportunity doesn't work out, they think of you the next time they have a critical role to fill. You want the HR person to like you.

- Beyond the interview, HR likes to be kept "in the loop." HR can become suspicious and defensive if it feels like it is being left out. When you correspond with the hiring manager, make sure you copy your contact in HR.

Another area where HR gets involved is during the offer process. When you get to this point, it's important to remember that HR isn't working for you; they are working for the company. You may think they have become your friend, but don't kid yourself. HR likes to show its value by keeping offers within the stated salary range, and if they can get someone to say "yes" for even less that is reason to celebrate. HR is an expense and likes to measure itself against the money it can save the company. Of course, that is short-sighted but understand what you are up against.

Always remember that HR people are rule followers, so you need to push hard for what you want. You also need to be clear about what you offer so you can get as close as possible to your asking price. The section on Internal Equity in Chapter 4 provides lots of examples and useful tips for navigating this part of the process.

Managers generally dislike working with HR because it is seen as an obstacle to solving business problems and filling an open position is a huge problem for any hiring manager. You need to convince the hiring manager that you have the skills, knowledge, and abilities they need so they will go to bat for you. Unless you have them as a strong ally, they will likely cave to the demands of HR.

Key Messages

It's important to play nice with HR. Regardless of how you feel about them, they can influence this process not in your favor. HR isn't your friend, so no matter how friendly they appear, they are often more concerned with their appearance and justifying their existence.

Remember with HR it's all about fit. Use your examples and stories to blend in the soft skills HR likes to hear about. Show adequate deference to help win HR over so they will advocate on your behalf. Most importantly, show respect by keeping them in the loop, even if the hiring manager doesn't seem interested in having them involved.

Coaching Questions

- What can you learn about the HR person you will deal with prior to the interview?

Searching For A Job Sucks!

- What are the top three soft skills you need to focus on during your interview with HR?

- What questions can you ask that shows you value their point of view?

Advice for Discouraged Job Seekers

I recently heard from an executive colleague who has been looking for a job for two years. I could hear the pain in his voice, and it broke my heart for two reasons. One, because I know he is extremely capable and only needs the right opportunity. Two, because I felt lost for words. What could I say that would bring comfort and hope to someone so desperate and clearly struggling? As my colleague said, "I never thought I would be in this place and not know how to fix it."

Searching for a job isn't easy. The longer it goes, the more difficult it seems to get and the scarier it becomes. In my experience, it can take professionals three to six months on average to find another job. TopResume noted the average job search can take five to six months. If you're employed, while it may be painful and inconvenient to wait, consider yourself fortunate. If you are unemployed, the experience can take much longer, and is much scarier and emotional.

There are several reasons why the time it takes can vary:

- The strength of the economy
- The growth or decline of your specific field
- The type of job you seek
- The number of open jobs
- The requirements for the role
- Your age
- Access to resources and tools to help with your search

Searching For A Job Sucks!

Most of these are variables you can't control, which makes the task even tougher.

So, What Can You Do?

If you are currently in this position and starting to get discouraged, there are several suggestions and questions you might want to ask yourself.

- Be realistic. Are you applying for roles that make sense, given your background and experience? Applying to fewer roles is an example where less can lead to more. Increasing your hit rate will reduce your level of frustration.

- Make an honest assessment. Is there something in your background or approach getting in the way? For example, is it poor tenure, a past employer's reputation, your age, the quality of your resume, the way you perform during an interview, and so on? You can't make this assessment by yourself. You need help from people willing to provide honest feedback. I recently had a Zoom call with someone before an interview and told him to smile more and show excitement. That one piece of advice helped him get past the first round of interviews.

- Make it easy for people to help. Do your friends, family, and colleagues know that you are looking? You can't ask them for a job, but you can ask periodically for advice and suggestions and networking referrals. You want to be top of mind if they hear about an opportunity you might like.

- Retool. Is it time to return to school to learn new skills that make you more marketable? School is expensive, so you'll want to be sure it's worth the investment.

- Stay current. Are you staying up to date in your chosen field by reading, attending conferences, or attending free webinars? Having this kind of knowledge will be helpful during an interview.

- Do what makes you happy. Are you pursuing something you love or something that only represents a paycheck? If so, this may be what you are projecting when you interview.

- Dial back expectations. Are you aiming too high or being too picky? Don't let your current lifestyle drive your job search. It may be time to adjust your lifestyle expectations so you can consider more possibilities.

- Assess the market. Is it time to consider relocating to an area of the country with more opportunities?

- Examine how you prepare for interviews. Do you engage in adequate research on the role, the company, and the industry? Can you share examples that demonstrate your ability to solve the problems they are facing?

- Walk away from your computer. Are you endlessly staring at your computer and not making progress? Get out into the real world and interact with people to keep your interpersonal skills sharp. Getting out also makes you feel better. Attend an association meeting, a networking event, and so on, and leave the house.

Searching For A Job Sucks!

- Review your resume. Does your resume describe your responsibilities, accomplishments, and unique capabilities well? Is it clear to the reader what you want to do next?

- Don't act desperate. Is it possible you come across as negative or hopeless when you network or during an interview? Stay positive by embracing what makes you special and being proud of your accomplishments.

- Job searching is like project management; it requires constant review and evaluation. Look closely at everything you are doing, and if it's not working, find ways to change your approach.

- Consider a coach. Would it help to have an expert resource assisting you with your job search? Having someone who can listen, push back, and offer helpful advice and encouragement can be beneficial.

- Stay in shape. Are you spending enough time getting exercise, and are you eating healthy? Exercise is an excellent mental and emotional break from your job search—set goals so you experience a sense of accomplishment.

- Use LinkedIn wisely. Are you spending countless hours on job boards? It has been reported that only 10% of jobs are found via job boards. LinkedIn gives you an opportunity to network and build relationships.

- Informational interviews. Do you wait to get an actual job interview before interviewing? Set up informational interviews so you are out in public and continue to learn. Meeting new and different people is a great way to expand your network.

- Focus on companies. Are you spending all of your time looking for open jobs? Switch gears and focus on specific companies where you know you can contribute. Find connections that can help you get your foot in the door.

- Don't focus on the job you didn't get. Do you find yourself consumed by regrets? Reflect on what you can learn and how you can improve and move forward.

- Reward yourself for small victories. Are you celebrating mini milestones to recognize your progress? Be kind to yourself. Eventually, these little victories will add up to a big win.

- Volunteer. Do you spend enough time helping others so you can take your mind off yourself? You might be surprised at what you learn and how good it makes you feel

- Take a break. Think of it as a mini vacation for two to three days. That may sound like odd advice if you are unemployed, but stepping away can clear your mind, provide a fresh perspective, and recharge the batteries. I know that when I tell myself to forget about a sticky problem, my subconscious continues to work, and seemingly, out of nowhere, I have a new idea.

My final advice may be the most important. Don't take this journey alone. If you have been searching unsuccessfully for a long time, this can be a lonely place, and it takes lots of emotional energy not to get discouraged and give up. Have you sought people willing to listen and can provide emotional support? Your local church might have a support group that you would find very helpful. Personal therapy with a counselor is another option. When you start to feel doubts and fears creeping in, reach out to a close friend for a coffee or dinner. Their words of support will take you a long way.

With that, take a deep breath, say a prayer, and despite how you feel and the circumstances, you are and will be okay.

Key Messages

The job search never goes as quickly as you would like. It seems to slow down even more when you start to interview. It's important to remain patient. Don't let anyone see you are anxious or desperate.

Take the time to reassess what you are doing and look for ways to improve. Ask people you trust for input and suggestions.

Searching for a job, especially when it is taking a long time, can be a lonely place. Don't take this journey alone. Build a support system for hope and encouragement.

You will never know for sure why someone didn't call you or why you didn't get a job. It's not always about you so don't assume the worst.

Coaching Questions

- If what you are doing isn't working, what could you do differently?

- Do you need to recalibrate your expectations?

- Are you spending enough time taking care of yourself?

CHAPTER 3: INTERVIEW - Why You Get Hired

What Comes after Rejection?

Rejection is part of looking for a job. You are not going to land every job you apply for— no one does!

So, What Can You Do?

Learning how to accept and respond to rejection and how to move forward is an important skill to develop. The following are some practical tips to help you look forward when you've just heard, "I'm sorry, it wasn't a good fit."

Take the High Road

Send a thank-you note. That's right. Even if you didn't get that job you really wanted, say thank you for the opportunity. Let them know you'd be interested if other opportunities become available in the future. Ask if it is okay to stay in touch and if they say "yes," make a point to reach out every six months. This is a classy move and will get you remembered. You can also ask for feedback, but don't be surprised if you don't get any. This isn't a process where employers can afford to be honest.

Don't Assume

There are many reasons why someone doesn't get hired; many of them have nothing to do with you. Maybe they hired an internal candidate, perhaps the successful candidate had an internal advocate, the job was posted to satisfy an HR requirement, and they already knew who they wanted to hire. Or, maybe you wore blue, and the interviewer had a traumatic experience as a child involving a clown dressed in blue. Why is it always about clowns? The point being this:

hiring is a very subjective, imperfect, and unpredictable process. As Doctor Phil likes to say, "It's not always about you!"

Keep in Touch

One of the best jobs I had in my career I got after initially being rejected; I stayed in touch. Every few months I would check in and provide a brief update on the work I was doing, my latest accomplishment, or comment on something I'd read about the organization. It took three years, but I finally got the offer I'd always wanted. To get what you want requires resilience and persistence. These are qualities you need to succeed in your career, and they leave a lasting impression on employers.

Conduct a Retrospective

It is important to reflect and to honestly ask yourself how you did. Did you dress appropriately, did you do enough research in advance to ask thoughtful questions to engage in conversation, did you answer the questions that were asked, did you show genuine excitement and interest in the job? Is it a job you were qualified for? Think of interviewing as a process that needs to be continually improved. While there is much of it you can't control, what you can control, you want to be great at.

Don't Give Up

There is an expression in sales that "every 'no' gets you closer to a 'yes'." The same is true when interviewing for a job. The only way you can succeed is by staying in the game. Do you really want to let them win? Marshall your competitive spirit and keep working. Learn from every experience, and eventually, the right opportunity will come along. As hard as it may be, let each rejection strengthen your resolve and make you more determined than ever. Giving up isn't an option!

Stay Positive

After lots of disappointment, staying positive is easier said than done. In the end, hiring is a very subjective process, and most times, hiring managers really don't know what they are looking for until they see it. To use a baseball metaphor: that is why you need lots of "at bats" to eventually land the right opportunity. This is how the process works, so don't get discouraged. You are still okay.

It's Out There

In all my years of recruiting, I can confidently say there is an opportunity out there for anyone who wants one. It just needs to be the right one. Sometimes finding the right one requires a recalibration of expectations. If you are willing to do that, the right opportunity will show itself eventually.

Key Messages

Rejection, whether you like it or not, is part of the process. With every rejection there is something to learn. I also believe every rejection gets you closer to "yes."

It's important to go after roles where you see a greater chance of being successful. Just because you think you can do a job doesn't mean you are the best person for the job.

Searching For A Job Sucks!

How you respond to rejection can build resiliency and persistence. Always take the high road and never assume is answer is no forever; it's just no for now. It's all about building relationships, so use this an opportunity to expand your connections.

Coaching Questions

- How do you respond to disappointment?
- How can you use disappointment to your advantage?
- What can you learn from the experience?

CHAPTER 3: INTERVIEW - Why You Get Hired

Lessons from Job Seekers

Don't Get Caught Off Guard

Paul is 25 years old and his first job out of college was selling computer hardware for a large reseller.

Paul was laid off as part of a large restructuring. He was caught off guard by the downsizing, so he had to start his search from square one.

He eventually found his new job by leveraging a connection at his former company who provided information about companies like his previous firm. One of these companies was founded by someone at his previous firm, and he reached out to an internal recruiter. This was a completely blind outreach that paid off.

In total, his search lasted six months. He took some time off initially and waited for about six weeks before he got serious about his search. He started by thinking long and hard about what he wanted to do next. He wasn't completely sure he wanted to go back to what he had been doing at his previous company. The idea of switching fields and doing something very different sounded exciting. He started by reaching out to alumni who were working in sports marketing or sports management. This had always been a dream and he thought that it could be a great field to transition into. As he learned more, he discovered entry-level jobs would be low paying and he had to decide if he was willing to make that trade-off. He also learned that getting an advanced degree would be another avenue for breaking into this field.

Searching For A Job Sucks!

Hearing these perspectives was very useful and helped him refocus his search.

The most challenging was staying motivated during the search. He was doing a lot of networking, completing applications, and reaching out to people he didn't know who might be able to help with his application.

Most of the time, he didn't get any responses. Keeping motivated when that happens can be discouraging. You need to understand there will be good days when you hear from people, but many other days when things are quieter, and you won't hear anything. Being in sales, he is used to hearing "no," but it still isn't easy.

One of his frustrations was aligning his schedule with the timetable of the hiring organizations. Some places have faster interview processes and others do not. Others take more time with multiple interviews that can take weeks to complete. He wished he had inquired about the next steps to understand the process and how long it would take. You need to know this when you are applying and interviewing for multiple roles.

He also learned not to fall in love with certain opportunities because it doesn't always turn out the way you hoped. The disappointment can be tough. Sometimes when things seem to be going well and you get too excited, it is easy to lose focus and not do the necessary preparation because you are expecting an offer. You need to be careful not to get too far ahead of yourself, regardless of what you think or are being told by a recruiter.

Upon reflection, Paul wonders what he could have done to avoid being caught off guard like he was. If he had looked at how his previous company was performing and the regular reorganizations, he would have realized some change was likely in the wind. He was very aware that the support resources he relied on to deliver quality to customers were significantly cut back, making his job much more difficult. He started to experience customers that were much less satisfied because he couldn't deliver the required level of service. He did initiate some interest in other internal roles, but the subsequent layoff occurred while he was interviewing. In retrospect, he should have also started to look externally.

When Paul's search was initially focused on sports marketing and sports management, he relied on his alumni network to make connections. These people connected him with other people not from his school, which greatly enhanced his network. That was a huge learning experience. Over 2 months, he had 20 to 30 conversations that helped him make critical decisions. He couldn't have learned all this by reading articles online.

Eventually, Paul pivoted and decided to stick with what he knew best and focused on tech sales. It was nice to step back into interviews where he understood the company's products and services and what they expected from candidates. Getting back to the familiar helped him appreciate how much he knows and reinforced his own capability. He was playing to his strengths, and it felt great! This was very different from trying to start over and facing the numerous trade-offs that transition required.

Looking back, he might not have taken so much time off after getting laid off. That said, the little break made it easier to dive into his search. Paul was adamant about saying a job search is a full-time job. You no longer have a manager holding you accountable or setting expectations. You need to do that yourself and that takes discipline. It took some time for Paul to adjust to the amount of time, effort and focus a successful job search requires. You need to treat the process with respect.

The biggest part of his process and what he learned was the value of networking. His job search became much more dependent on working with other people, and that was something he never realized when he was coming out of college. His recommendation is to reach out to people, even if you don't think they will get back to you. He learned from numerous conversations that many people ended up in their current role because someone else helped them along the way, and given the opportunity, they will pay it forward. When someone reaches out to them, they know exactly what it's like to look for a job and want to help if they can. Many people are willing and open to help, so don't go it alone.

What Happens in Vegas…Doesn't Always Stay in Vegas

Sam is a 48-year-old executive who has spent most of his career in sales for large, well-known consumer products companies. Most recently, he became a company president for the first time.

Sam found himself looking for a new job when he and the owner at his previous company disagreed on the future direction of the company. After lots of conversation, they parted on good terms. Sam left in May and took some time off to deal with personal matters. He started to get organized in August and launched his job search in September.

CHAPTER 3: INTERVIEW - Why You Get Hired

Sam started by getting his LinkedIn up to date and by reaching out to the top of his network.

Sam shared upfront that he isn't a good networker. Going to events and shaking lots of hands isn't something Sam finds enjoyable or comfortable. Having to tell his story over and over is exhausting.

Sam was fortunate to have an immediate network of friends and colleagues he could reach out to. He had cultivated this network over the years, not necessarily to fall back on, but when he reached out, he was fortunate that people got back to him. For Sam, these were easy calls or notes to send. This is absolutely where you want to start when you engage in networking. Sam would have been lost had he not taken the time to stay close to a core group of close individuals throughout his career. However, Sam also made the point that it wasn't until he got to the second level of his network that his networking became productive. This is important to note as it is often true of networking. The conversations with his immediate connections, as well as with other acquaintances he didn't know as well, led to more and more conversations. Sam found himself having 15 to 20 conversations a week.

Never in these conversations did he ask anyone for a job. Sam solicited their input on job search strategies, recruiters they knew, thoughts about the marketplace, what he should think about most importantly, whom they knew who might have additional insight he would find helpful. This is how the roots and his network continued to expand.

Sam ended each call with an offer to help. In his mind, people have been gracious with their time, so he wanted to return the favor. This often led to a conversation about the challenges they were facing, and Sam was able to share his insight and expertise. Offering to help further strengthened the relationship.

Sam describes the greatest challenge of his job search as being mental. Sam was fortunate; he had received a good severance package and had savings to fall back on, so money wasn't his great worry. At the peak of his search, he worked four to six hours a day, and all the phone calls were exhausting. After talking with 150 people or so, Sam explained that it starts to mess with your head. He knew the search would be slow, but he didn't know it would be this slow. You need to have a playbook and follow the process. For Sam, the responsiveness of people is what carried him through. It can be a lonely place with lots of ups and downs.

What he found most frustrating was how recruiters treated him. Sam learned very early in the process, and this is important for everyone to hear, that he is the product, not the client. Sam would have a good initial call with a recruiter who said they liked his background and would get back to him, and he would hear nothing. They wouldn't return calls or emails; he was ghosted.

After hearing nothing from the recruiter for weeks or months, the recruiter would show up a month later, and say they have something that isn't right for you, but they are wondering who you know. He learned very quickly that he was only a source and there was very little interest in having a relationship. If a recruiter needs something from you, they will talk to you. If not, they won't have time.

Sam would often ask a recruiter what he could do to help the recruiter tell his story better.

CHAPTER 3: INTERVIEW - Why You Get Hired

This is a great way to help a recruiter and to make their job easier.

Searching for a job often feels like a roller coaster, and Sam learned not to get too excited about any one opportunity. Having been on the inside, Sam knows how long it can take to fill a job and how many things can go wrong along the way.

Hands down, the best advice Sam received was to know exactly what he was looking for. This is the work you do before starting to search and talk to anyone. What kind of role are you looking for, what industry, what size company, and what kind of culture and management style? That becomes the center of your bullseye, so you know what trade-offs you are willing to make. You need to know yourself and what you need to be successful and happy. Once Sam understood this, it didn't change much during his search.

Starting this process, Sam struggled with the idea that anyone would be willing to help him. This was another of the mental hurdles. He had low expectations, but people he hadn't spoken to in eight years jumped in and were willing to help. The eye-opener for Sam was how much more fruitful his second tier of contacts proved to be. This expanded his network beyond what he thought possible.

Sam points out that you can't pass along your tension or anxiety. You don't want people to feel the weight of your challenge if you are in a rough place. This is often a red flag for a recruiter or hiring manager, if someone comes across as too desperate. They want to hire people who are calm under fire, confident that they can overcome any challenge they face.

Searching For A Job Sucks!

Sam also acknowledges that everyone's experience is different. Some people will tell you that networking is a waste of time. Others will tell you not to bother with recruiters. You have to figure out what works for you. Job boards were part of his playbook, but were far less fruitful. Rather than apply online, Sam would reach out directly to the director or hiring manager to introduce himself, and this resulted in more conversations. Ultimately, you have to get comfortable knowing that you will do 1,000 things, and only one will pay off in the end.

Sam offered a final piece of advice that may be the most important for job seekers. Sam would tell job seekers that if they knew when this would be over, they could have much more fun. You can spend only so much time a day looking for a job. For Sam, that was four hours a day. Otherwise, you will drive yourself crazy. If you are unemployed and looking for a job, use this as a time to spend more time with your family, volunteer, exercise, and so on. Take time for yourself and use the time to re-energize.

After four months, Sam was close to a couple of opportunities when a cousin convinced him to take time away from his job search and go to Vegas to celebrate his birthday. On his last night there, Sam decided to play craps one last time. While playing, he struck up a conversation with someone at the table who was from the same town. This person happened to be the founder of a company that Sam knew was looking to hire a new president. He knew this because he had spoken to a recruiter several times but had never gotten an introduction. After exchanging contact information and agreeing to meet when they got home, Sam was offered the job within a month, after several conversations and meeting other team members.

The lesson here is simple: you never know when opportunity will show itself. Being curious about anyone you meet with a desire to listen and learn can open doors you never thought possible.

Companies Only Care When They Are Hiring

Allan is 35 years old and has been a development engineer/architect for 11 years with a focus on Software as a service (SaaS) applications. He has worked for several firms and has been working remotely long before the pandemic.

Allan started to see red flags where he worked, so started to apply for jobs. Before he was able to find anything new, he was part of a 20% reduction in force. As one of the most expensive employees, he wasn't surprised to be on the chopping block.

Allan's job search was about three-months long—from the end of October to the end of January. He thought it would go quicker, but Christmas slowed down his search.

Most challenging for Allan was getting one hard "no" after thinking the interviewing process for a role had gone fantastic. He learned that you never really know what to expect when you interview.

Staying motivated and managing time was most difficult for Allan. The interviewing process is different everywhere, and most companies want you to spend at least three hours interviewing. He learned to be patient and to manage his schedule so he could take 30-minute interviews.

For the job he received, he had a 30-minute interview with an internal recruiter, a one-hour technical screen, and three more interviews, including another tech screen. He described this as the best interviewing process he had experienced.

One company that wanted him to interview gave him a take-home assignment that was far too large a piece of work, and he viewed this as a red flag and an indication of unrealistic expectations of their developers. He believes that companies should pay you if they are asking you to do more than two hours of work.

Allan will say there is no silver bullet. He has had five jobs in his career. His first three jobs he knew people at the company, and they brought him in to interview and he was hired. The last two jobs were merit-based, and he had to prove his problem-solving capabilities and business acumen in a very short window. Allan applied to the company that hired him, twice, for two different roles. The first time he was told they had a hiring freeze. He went back a few weeks later and found another job that looked interesting. This is the job he was offered.

Being persistent and applying frequently and going back and looking at what new jobs have been posted were the key to his success. Allan describes hiring as a black-box timing game. Companies don't care when you are looking for a job; they only care when they are hiring. It's when the stars align in this very narrow window that the magic happens.

Allan's advice is both to pray and look in lots of different places. In his experience, better jobs come from internal recruiters and applying directly.

CHAPTER 4: OFFER

Beware of Internal Equity

You don't know how compensation works if you don't understand internal equity. For example, if you have been with your current organization longer than two or three years, there is a good chance you are underpaid. As hard as you work, I'll bet you liked hearing that! The job market is almost always moving faster than internal compensation structures. The longer you stay in any one place, the further you fall behind. That isn't always a wrong choice if the other trade-offs make sense. However, don't kid yourself; this is one serious downside to longevity. You severely limit your earning potential.

Most medium- to larger-sized organizations rely on compensation structures to determine their pay for a given role. These are usually based on market intelligence and reflect what other organizations pay for a similar role. Not only are these compensation studies out of date the moment they are published, but they also focus on what most people in each job get paid. Without inferring too much about the statistics, that sounds like an average or median. So, if you think of yourself as an average performer, that's what you can expect to get paid—no more, and after a while, likely less. And guess what? The more an organization can pay you like an average employee, the happier they are. How do you like being thought of as average?

Searching For A Job Sucks!

So far, the conversation about compensation has been about "roles?" Not once have I ever used the word *person*. That's because compensation structures focus on roles and not the people they are trying to hire and what they are worth. If you consider yourself more than average, why would you want to be limited by a compensation structure designed to control costs and align with the market versus hiring the best talent? Stated another way, compensation structures are designed to maintain the status quo.

If you see an organization with lots of tenured employees, be wary. They are likely to offer substandard wages compared to the market. As such, the offers they extend will reflect their desire to maintain internal pay equity and won't necessarily reflect what you are worth. While incumbents have chosen to stay, probably for personal reasons, it should raise a red flag for anyone entertaining an offer from such an organization. They are likely to offer lower wages compared to the market. You need to know your industry and what's happening with wages. You can ask for more when there is a high demand for scarce talent.

An example of this today is the accounting field. Fewer students are going to school for accounting, fewer people are taking the CPA exams, and the grind of public accounting doesn't align with what people expect from their employers in this post-COVID environment. Firms without well-known brand names have no choice but to pay more for talent. If they don't and are more concerned about maintaining internal equity, you may want to look elsewhere.

Understanding the connection between internal equity and building wealth for yourself is essential. The only way to achieve a step function increase is by changing companies. The compensation philosophy at most organizations is simple—pay as much as necessary and as little as possible. The longer you stay with any organization, the more your income is gated by that way of operating.

I recently had the head of recruiting ask me to ask a candidate how little they would need to accept a role. Is that a place you want to work?

So, What Can You Do?

The lesson here is simple. Leadership doesn't care about your ability to generate wealth; leadership only cares about the bottom line, the ability to satisfy shareholders if they are a publicly traded company, and what that means for their annual bonus. So, how does that align with your ability to build wealth, support your family, and achieve your desired lifestyle?

Much attention is given to what CEOs earn versus the typical worker. In an article for Economic Policy Institute, Lawrence Mishel and Jori Kandra reported that CEO pay has skyrocketed 1,322% since 1978. The article explains that "CEOs were paid 351 times as much as a typical worker in 2020." That isn't an issue I will tackle here, but it might give you more to inquire about when you are interviewing for a job.

As you may know, executive-level compensation for publicly traded companies is all public information published quarterly in their 10-Q; the Securities and Exchange Commission (SEC) requires these reports. For a moment, forget about CEO pay, but look at the compensation for the CEO's direct reports. You want to focus on the gap between those roles and the ones that report into them. If you see a vast discrepancy between those numbers and what you are currently earning or what you might make if offered a job, you need to consider if this is an offer you want to accept. As an executive recruiter, I know firsthand that executives do a great job taking care of themselves, but there is often a considerable gap at the levels below. Don't forget the prevailing reality about compensation philosophy: pay as much as you have to, but as little as possible. If you choose to work for this company, which might make sense for many reasons, just realize you are working to make others wealthy and sacrificing your ability to build wealth.

There is also another aspect of compensation that is important to understand. Your value in the marketplace is often determined by what you are making.

When a recruiter or hiring organization asks you about your current compensation, which they shouldn't be doing, they are attempting to make at least two judgments:

1. What is your level of capability compared to others in a similar role?

2. How much will it take for you to accept an offer? Stated another way, how low will you go?

Fair or not, recruiters and hiring managers will sometimes decide if you are qualified for a job based on your compensation. This is the clear downside of sharing compensation information with a recruiter or hiring manager. If you are fortunate enough to receive an offer, it will likely be based on whatever you tell them. That number might be very different from your actual value in the marketplace or how you view your own capability. I believe this is one of the reasons the compensation for women has historically been less than men and continues to lag men. I'll have more to say on that topic latter.

You also may have to ask yourself when/if it make sense to take a step back financially for what might seem to be a great career opportunity? Sometimes, the answer is "yes," but it's not a decision to take lightly. Accepting a lower starting salary because of a "great" opportunity is something you want to consider very seriously.

When faced with this decision, it's important to calculate how long it will take to make up what you are losing in base salary. Let's say your current base salary is $100,000 and you are offered that "dream" job at $85,000. According to an October 17, 2023, press release by the Conference Board, companies raised their budgets for employee salary increases by 4.4% in 2023. If you figure a 4.4% salary increase against a base salary of $85,000, it will take you four years to make up what you have lost. If you stay in our current job for four years, your base salary would now be over $116,000. The fact is, you never catch up unless you get another large increase along the way. That is why you need to ask yourself if that "job you've always wanted" will pay off in the longer term.

A 2023 article titled "When Should You Take a Pay Cut?" asks the reader the following three questions that are worth considering before taking a pay cut. There is no right or wrong answer. As the article stated, "It's a personal decision about what matters most to you and how it will impact your life now and in the long run."

Searching For A Job Sucks!

1. Will you be able to afford your current standard of living? What changes will you need to make, if any?

2. What other benefits, perks, or compensation are you being offered?

3. Will this job open up more or better opportunities for growth and/or earning long-term?

So, unless the thought of Monday morning generates dread and anxiety and you are miserable in your job, you want to think carefully about accepting an offer from a company that requires you to take a step back financially. You need to ask yourself if taking a pay cut will make that feeling even worse. Your current financial obligations will still be your financial obligations. You need to be sure the concessions are worthwhile.

It is crucial to think of your career as an investment. In this case, it is an investment in yourself. It may be the most important investment you ever make. Therefore, you need to consider the longer implications of taking a step back to take a significant move forward. Here are nine possible examples where it might make sense:

1. You can join a widely known, highly regarded organization. I often tell people to work for the most well-known, highly regarded brand they can. The organization you work for matters and can open other doors that otherwise may have been closed. Other organizations will find you interesting based on where you have worked before.

2. You see many opportunities to learn new skills that make you more marketable. Continuing to learn and develop is the key to

CHAPTER 4: OFFER - Beware of Internal Equity

any successful career. You want to stack your portfolio with as much expertise as you possibly can. That's what organizations pay for.

3. Being offered significant equity in exchange for cash is another possibility worth considering. But, again, these are high-risk, high-reward opportunities and may not work out. If it doesn't and you need to look for another job, most employers will understand.

4. You see many possibilities for advancement—ideally sooner than later. So maybe this is the way to get your foot in the door. In other words, a shorter-term trade-off for a longer-term payoff. That can make lots of sense.

5. You are trying to enter a new industry or changing fields. However, your value in this instance is diminished because you have not demonstrated the required skills or knowledge or have the necessary track record of accomplishments.

6. More experienced professionals—code for older—may face this question later in their careers. For some, this is often more of a lifestyle issue and may require a step back to stay engaged in the workforce. If you are at the point where you want to keep busy, and money isn't the primary objective, taking a lower salary makes a lot of sense.

7. There is another reason that cuts right to the heart of the matter— you want to stay employed. Being paid less is sometimes better than not being paid at all. If you see the writing on the wall and

Searching For A Job Sucks!

layoffs are eminent, consider asking for a severance package and jump to the new opportunity.

8. We have all seen that post-pandemic, many professionals are in search of more flexibility. Better work-life balance has become a higher priority. If taking a pay cut translates into more time to do what you want or need to do, it might make sense.

9. It may also be you are seeking more fulfillment in your work. I have seen people leave a corporate job and go to work for not-for-profit organizations where they feel an emotional connection to the mission. Not-for-profit organizations will often offer less in base salary, but you may see an increase in the benefits. We all know that money can't buy happiness, especially if earning more makes you miserable.

Knowing the challenges associated with compensation, how can you position yourself for the best offer possible?

For starters, don't share your current compensation with a recruiter or hiring manager. As soon as you share this information, you open the door to an offer that pays less than what you currently earn. You most definitely invite an offer that is less than what you think you are worth. If you have been with an organization for several years and are likely being paid below market, you have the potential to receive a significant increase.

You don't want an offer limited by an internal compensation structure. Company compensation professionals worry about internal equity and keeping everyone in the same job paid relatively the same. One colleague shared that the 11th commandment at his company was "Thou shall not violate internal equity." When many people in the same role are paid about the same, it's called compensation compression. Organizations don't worry about compensation compression until top talent starts walking out the door. Until then, they are pleased to pay you as little as you will accept.

For women, this is a very relevant issue. A Pew Research Center article by Carolina Aragão reported, "The gender gap in pay has remained relatively stable in the United States over the past 20 years or so." Telling a recruiter or hiring manager what you are earning perpetuates the problem. You want a recruiter or hiring manager to base their evaluation on the skills, knowledge, ability, and what you can potentially contribute, not on wages that are very likely below market.

In October 2017, California Governor Jerry Brown signed Assembly Bill 168, prohibiting employers from asking job applicants for their salary history. If an applicant requests, employers are required to provide a salary range. The Shouse Law Group reported in an article titled "Can California Employers Ask Job Applicants about Salary History?":

"Salary history can reinforce pay inequality based on sex, race, or other types of discrimination. Employers can use salary history to pay some employees less than others. Prohibiting questions about salary history is a way to compensate employees based on job skills and experience."

I think it won't be long before this becomes the law of the land. HR Dive updated its list of states and localities on August 2, 2023, which

Searching For A Job Sucks!

outlawed pay history questions. The states and the date their statewide bans were enacted are listed as follows:

Alabama—9/1/2019

California—1/12018

Colorado—1/1/2001

Connecticut—1/1/2019

Delaware—12/14/2017

District of Columbia—11/17/2017

Hawaii—1/12019

Illinois—1/15/2019

Maine—1/17/2019

Maryland—1/10/2020

Massachusetts—7/1/2018

Minnesota—1/1202

Missouri – 2019

Nevada—10/1/2021

New Jersey—2/1/2020

New York—1/9/2020

North Carolina—4/2/2019

Oregon—10/6/2017

Puerto Rico—3/8/2017

Rhode Island—1/12023

Vermont—1/7/2018

Washington—7/28/2019

Even if you live in a state where it isn't illegal, it's time to stop sharing what you currently earn. So, what do you do if you are asked

CHAPTER 4: OFFER - Beware of Internal Equity

this question? Unless you live in one of the states from the preceding list, don't be surprised if someone asks you this question.

An article by Lila Gaylor, Manager, Recruiting Services in Houston, Texas, advised hiring managers on how to get around this restriction. The advice was to "tweak your salary question." Rather than ask someone what they made in their last job, ask, "What are your salary expectations for this position?"

In most cases, if you are being asked this question upfront in the recruiting process, realistically, how can you possibly know? A job offer consists of much more than a base salary. Don't get drawn into answering this question early in the process; you may miss out on a great opportunity. The best answer is to deflect and let the hiring manager or recruiter know you can answer that question after you learn more.

Whatever you do, don't offer a range. Many job seekers think they give themselves some flexibility by providing a range and won't eliminate themselves from consideration. However, how often do you think an employer would reach the top of a candidate's range? "Never" is the answer. You can always expect an offer at the lower end of the stated range. When you balk at the offer, the employer will act confused and even a little annoyed as they met the indicated range.

The alternative is to tell your potential employer that what you earn currently has no bearing on the job you are applying for because it is a different job, titles from one company to another don't always mean the same thing, the culture isn't the same, the industry might be different, geography, or whatever. You want to know how a prospective employer evaluates your capability and potential, and you would expect them to extend an offer based on that if they are interested. If they continue to press and refuse to proceed without you sharing this personal information, you need to ask yourself if this is where you want to work.

Another way to approach this is to say compensation is negotiable based on many other factors, including benefits, bonuses, equity, perks, and job responsibilities. For example, would you ever tell a car salesperson how much you would pay for a car before seeing, driving, doing online research, and looking under the hood? Okay, maybe you don't look under the hood to see a computer but otherwise, of course not! So why should you commit to a potential salary before knowing everything about the company and the role?

Knowing all that, you can expect many companies will press hard for a number. That's well and good, but what you want is for the organization to put its number on the table first. Smart organizations that truly value talent will do this, so they don't waste anyone's time. Those that don't are ones you want to watch out for. They are trying to get you on the cheap. You might try asking them what the range is for a particular position. If they continue to press (this is why your research is so critical), you can state something around $XYZ might make sense for a role like this in this location, industry, and with this title, but you'd like to learn more before committing. As I said before, be wary of organizations that operate this way and remember what they are trying to do. They want to fit you into their internal equity structure regardless of your skills and ability. Given alternatives, is this really where you want to work?

One way to get ahead of this, before investing lots of time and effort is to ask upfront about the salary. This was frowned on in the past,

CHAPTER 4: OFFER - Beware of Internal Equity

but as a recruiter, I would rather get this on the table earlier than later so I don't waste anyone's time. If a recruiter or hiring manger doesn't want to share this information upfront I would be wary about what you can expect. You simply want to know you are in the ballpark before investing lots of time and emotional energy in the process. And, if they turn the question around and ask what you expect, fall back on your research to offer a number.

Job seekers need to understand that most employers prefer not to negotiate for salary. However, there is often wiggle room that you don't want to leave on the table. Remember, employers don't want to overpay, and if they can hire a talented person and pay below market, why not try? It is definitely okay to ask, and again, this is where your research can be helpful. You can say that based on what you know about this kind of work, you would like to see ABC as the offer. Negotiating for salary is normal and almost expected.

I spoke with a colleague recently who told me a company that wanted to hire him asked him to suggest a starting salary. After doing some research and giving it thought, he returned with a number that he thought was fair and motivating.

The response was interesting and one to watch. The answer was this —that number is higher than we hope to pay. Can you come back with another number as we'd really like you to join the team.

Stop right there and recognize what is about to happen. You are now negotiating against yourself in a rapid race to the bottom. What the company is actually asking, and what you should hear, is the following: "How little will you take?"

Searching For A Job Sucks!

This story illustrates several lessons worth noting:

- The best time to negotiate your salary is when you are offered a job, so don't squander the opportunity. This is when you have the most leverage.

- If you want to negotiate, you must be willing to walk away; otherwise, it isn't a negotiation. It is critical to know your walkaway number. At some point, you must decide if this company is worthy of your talents. You may have achieved your limit of what's possible after a couple of rounds.

- Don't expect more than a couple of rounds.

- Know your financial situation and value in the marketplace so you don't undersell yourself.

- If you do get asked for a number and they won't back off, aim high. Position your request based on the following:

    o The requirements of the job and everything they expect

    o The very relevant experience you bring to the role

    o The ability to make an immediate contribution

    o Where the job is located and cost of living

- Don't lowball yourself. You can't be ridiculous with your ask, but offer the number that would excite you if they said "yes." If they want you, force them to come back with a number.

CHAPTER 4: OFFER - Beware of Internal Equity

- Don't ever tell them what you make. If they press, you may eventually have to, but remember, this is about the future, not the past. Focus on what you are worth, what you expect, and why. Know the market for your industry, discipline, and experience so you can bring relevant data to the conversation.

- Most importantly, under no circumstances should you start negotiating against yourself when an organization keeps asking what it will take after you've already told them what it will take. Remember, this is code for how low will you go. Ask them to make the best offer they possibly can. Tell them you don't know enough about their compensation system and salary bands to know what to expect. Plead innocent to what a role like this might pay in a company their size.

- The goal is to get them to show their cards first. They can put together a compelling offer if they want you badly. If they aren't willing to do that, how badly do you want to work for them?

The key for job seekers is to do their homework. I am not a fan of public websites where you can allegedly find salary information. I won't name names, but highly successful and highly compensated professionals rarely visit these sites—they don't have time! What you often find are people with an axe to grind. These are not the reference points you want to use when making salary decisions.

Your best bet is to call people you know doing well in comparable roles, in the same industry and geography and get their input. I would not ask the salary question in an email or text; that might seem too intrusive, but first, try to connect based on shared backgrounds and experiences. You can use LinkedIn to find people that can help you.

Searching For A Job Sucks!

Is there an alum you can reach out to who can help? Do you know a recruiter you can ask? Is there someone you know who might be able to find the right person for you to contact? Ask them what they would expect a job like XYZ at a Company like ABC to pay? To say to a prospective employer that, based on your research, a comparable job is worth XYZ puts you in a better position to ask for what you want.

As I've already stated, compensation is more than the base salary. For example, it is sometimes easier to get additional equity than a higher base salary if the offer involves equity. Another option is a sign-on bonus. That is a one-time cost and more manageable for an organization to absorb. Ensure they gross up the amount, so you aren't stuck with all the taxes and a sign-on that is reduced by 30% to 40%.

You need to know something else that may escape the average job seeker. Most organizations have job families with associated compensation ranges for each role. Your task as a job seeker is to learn that structure, and it isn't that difficult. For example, let's say you are interviewing for the marketing manager job. You want to ask how many levels are above and below the marketing coordinator role and the compensation ranges. Once you know this, you can ask for the compensation you'd like to receive. For example, you may learn that the position you are considering is much more junior than you thought. On the other hand, you may see a way to ask for the top-of-the-range and inquire about the opportunities for promotion.

You find this out by asking. You couch the question in your desire to learn about growth opportunities. Most employers will respond favorably and likely share the information.

Key Messages

You will never have more leverage to increase your compensation than during the hiring process. Know your worth and the market and lobby for as much as you can possibly get. Remember that companies will pay you as much as they have to and as little as possible.

Never tell a recruiter or hiring manager your current compensation. Knowing this is how companies hold you back. You want to be paid on your value and what you can contribute. Watch out for the organization that wants you to negotiate against yourself.

If you are considering a step back financially, do the math and make sure it makes sense. As unfair as it might seem, you are often valued in the marketplace by what you make.

Coaching Questions

- How much do you know about a company's compensation structure?
- What does the market tell you about your worth?
- How will any given offer impact the other priorities in your life?

Buyer Beware

There is nothing more exciting than getting a job offer! It is both affirming and exhilarating. After many anxious weeks or months of hard work, it can be a huge relief. It is time to grab your favorite beverage and celebrate!

After receiving an offer, it is also the time to remind yourself that the interviewing process flows both ways. These can be life-changing decisions, so it is crucial to have all the data you can before deciding to say "yes."

If you haven't considered this in the past, once you receive an offer, the burden falls on you to make a wise decision. While organizations want to learn as much about you as they possibly can, they will hide or at least omit everything they can about themselves that might make them less desirable. I'm not suggesting they lie, but if you don't ask, they won't tell. And even when you do, the truth will be shaded to their advantage.

To avoid unwanted surprises, you need to gather enough data to make an informed decision. That starts with being adequately prepared for an interview, but that is probably your least reliable source of information.

So, What Can You Do?

You need to start by going outside of the interviewing process to gather confirming or disconfirming data. You may have done some of this work to prepare for your interviews, but if not, now is the time to start. For starters, speak with current and or former employees you can trust, read about the industry and future forecasts, research what industry experts are saying about the organization, find out about voluntary and involuntary turnover and if they are publicly traded, review the financial information in annual reports and 10Ks and look for private investments in the company on sites like TechCrunch, listen to analyst calls to understand challenges the organization might be facing, and look on sites like Vault.com to see top-ranked companies. You can also look on sites like Glassdoor, but that is considered by many as a great place for disgruntled employees, past and present, to bitch and moan, so you be the judge.

Beyond the questions you want to ask about culture, which are covered in another chapter, there are questions about the role and the organization that are equally important to ask and get answered.

Use your research to form a complete, unbiased view of your potential employer. The adage "trust but verify" offers great guidance on how to proceed during the interviewing process and after you receive an offer.

The following questions will help you gather the data you need to make an informed decision. Ellie Richards wrote a September 18, 2023, article for Vault that provides a helpful list of questions (https://vault.com/blogs/job-search/10-things-to-check-before-accepting-a-job-offer). What questions you ask will be determined by the position you have been offered and who you are speaking to. If you didn't hear answers to these questions during the interviewing process, you will want them now.

Searching For A Job Sucks!

Why is the position open?

Was the incumbent promoted? Did they leave voluntarily or involuntarily? How long were they in the role? What happened to the person in this role before the incumbent?

How long has the position been open?

If the position has been open longer than three months, why is that? What makes this hard to fill?

What has the turnover in this role been like in the last 24 to 36 months?

How many people have passed through this role? Dig in to find out why.

Why have people failed in the past?

Are the reasons all related to the employee or does the organization acknowledge some responsibility? Be careful if it's all on the employee and there has been repeated turnover in the same role.

What kind of onboarding support exists?

Is there a clear plan and process that extends beyond the first day?

How do current employees help new employees be successful?

If someone can't answer this question in detail, expect to be left on your own to sink or swim.

What do employees think of the person who will be your boss?

Ask your interviewers if they would work for this person if they had the opportunity.

If I don't hear an immediate resounding "yes" to this question, you need to probe more deeply and understand why. As is seen in the next chapter, these may be the most important questions you ask.

How often do layoffs occur?

If the answer you hear is frequently, you better think twice. Organizations love to talk about themselves as one big family, but, as I noted before, when was the last time you downsized a family member?

If there was a recent layoff, why did it occur?

Was there a clear explanation provided by leadership? What does the answer tell you about the future of the enterprise? Did leadership accept any responsibility for the layoff?

How close is the actual culture to what you see described on the website?

We cover this extensively in another part of the book. Understanding the culture is an important question to get answered and requires many questions to truly understand what you are getting into.

How do people feel about the company's leadership?

Do they demonstrate concern for employee satisfaction while still expecting high performance and holding people accountable? Do they respect them as leaders? Would they follow someone if they left and went to another organization?

How does leadership allow flexibility for employees?

How much flexibility will you have to determine where and how you work? What has leadership indicated about the future of the workplace?

How often do you see fire drills, and how do people respond?

You see who people are in times of crisis. How does the leadership team respond to problems that require immediate attention? Is the organization in constant chaos? What is the environment like on a day-to-day basis?

How does the organization support training and development opportunities?

It doesn't matter if the organization has continuous training and development programs if you can't take advantage of them. How often are people allowed to get offline to pursue such opportunities? Is this on your time or the company's time? What kind of support is available to pursue advanced degrees?

Does the company operate in a growing market?

It is essential to understand what is happening in the broader marketplace. You need to step away from the job you are pursuing and learn about the bigger picture. Is the market growing, shrinking, or stagnant? If the market isn't growing or projected to grow, does this mean you could soon be looking for another job?

How does the product and or service stand up against the competition?

What do customer reviews tell you about the product or service? How do industry experts rank it? How does the competition compare? Is it something you can get excited about even if you can't or won't be a user

How do the benefits offered compare to other organizations?

You don't want to evaluate an offer on annual compensation only. You must consider total compensation—base salary, bonus, equity, benefits, and so on. How does the total compensation compare to what you are leaving? Is there an opportunity to ask for more based on what you may be leaving behind? Is the offer compelling, lateral, or even worse, less than what you make now? Does it make sense to take a cut, and if so, why?

How often does the company promote from within versus looking outside?

Companies love to talk about growth opportunities, but I see organizations that hire a lot from the outside. That happens because an organization will always know more about a current employee than they ever will about any outside candidate. I'm talking about everything good about them, but also every mistake, perceived weakness, and personality quirk. Knowing all this can put internal candidates at a decided disadvantage. Look for a track record to determine what growth opportunities exist.

What metrics will be used to evaluate my performance, and what does success look like?

Do employees understand what is expected and what "great" looks like? Do they have regular one-on-ones with their manager to assess progress, receive coaching, and make corrections?

How often will I be reviewed?

Is there a process in place to review performance? How often does it occur? Do employees find it helpful? Do employees find the review process fair?

The goal is to unearth helpful insight that helps you make an informed decision. While you can also ask these questions during an interview, don't always trust what you hear. Unfortunately, when responding to your questions, most interviewers are either unprepared, tell you what you want to hear, don't feel comfortable being honest or don't know. It is up to the person being interviewed to gather good data that leads to an intelligent decision.

As you are listening, look for answers that are consistent from person to person and the themes that are forming. Watch how someone reacts to your question. Are they uncomfortable, are they hedging, are they answering the question you asked? Use your external research to corroborate what you hear internally. The contradictions tell you where to dig deeper.

I suspect you've been told at some point in your professional career that you are interviewing them as much as they are interviewing you. While that is true, most candidates don't ask the right questions and fail to uncover essential data points that can lead to failure. The goal is to avoid surprises and make a smart decision based on as many facts as possible. After that, you make the best judgment call you can and move forward confident in your decision.

Key Messages

Don't assume that the company making an offer is being honest about their reality.

You need to do adequate due diligence to know how the company is actually performing. The Balance Sheet, Cash Flow Statement and Income statement are a good place to start. Some of this you may need to ask for if the company isn't publicly traded. You can also listen to the most recent earnings call to see what the analysts who follow the company are saying.

Outside of the numbers, look for people who will tell you the truth and listen carefully to what they say and don't say. This is your opportunity to ask tough questions.

Ultimately, it's 100% on you to make smart, well-informed decision. You will probably never know everything that's going on but you want to avoid huge surprises.

Coaching Question

- What matters most to you in this new role?

- What themes do you hear and see as you talk to people and review the numbers?

- What do you need to do differently in the future to avoid being surprised?

Searching For A Job Sucks!

The New Boss

I have touched on this topic briefly in the previous chapter, but it's so important it deserves much more attention. For many job seekers, this may be the most critical chapter in the book. Why? The relationship with your potential new boss can determine your ultimate success and overall satisfaction with your choice. When the relationship is strong, it's incredible. When it's not, the outcome can be a complete derailment.

As much as you may want a particular job, you must ensure a solid emotional and intellectual connection with the hiring manager. There are two ways to figure that out. The first is your firsthand experience with the hiring manager during the interviewing process and their answers to your questions. Consider this your primary or firsthand research. Engaging your head, heart, and gut is essential as you conduct this research.

So, What Can You Do?

First, pay attention to your experience with the hiring manager. For example:

- Was the hiring manager excited to meet you?
- Were they on time?
- Did they seem prepared for the interview?
- Did they take adequate time to get to know you?
- Did they avoid interruptions?

CHAPTER 4: OFFER - Beware of Internal Equity

- Were they as interested in your questions as their own?
- Did you get sufficient time to ask your questions?
- Did you get the opportunity to have more than one meeting?
- Are they able to make a crisp decision?

The lesson here is simple: what you see is what you get. Don't overthink and wish it were something different.

Next, you need the hiring manager to address expectations associated with the job. For example:

- Do you understand the work you will be doing?
- Is there a clear understanding of how success will be measured?
- Do you know the group or department's culture and how people work together?
- Do you agree on the title?
- Is there agreement on how much time you will spend in the office versus working from home or remotely?

You want to leave this interview confidently and excited about the role and the work.

And finally, what do you think of the hiring manager?

- Do you like them as a person?

Searching For A Job Sucks!

- Is their management style a good fit with how you like to work?

- Can you learn from this person?

- Do they talk about others or only themselves?

If you don't feel any chemistry, ask yourself if this is the right fit. Your gut will guide you to the right decision.

You don't want to be surprised and disappointed after starting a new job. Gathering this type of data is critical to your decision-making process.

The other type of research, which is equally critical, is secondhand research. Looking outside the formal interviewing process can help you gather additional data about your potential new boss. If you are favorably impressed during your primary research, you need this to calibrate your reaction. You need both affirmation and contrary evidence to make an informed decision.

Start by creating a list of friends and colleagues who might know this person. Maybe they have worked for this person or have other friends and colleagues who have worked for this person. If and when you find these people, there is only one question you need to ask, and I'll repeat it from the previous chapter: "If given the opportunity, would you work with or for this person again." You are looking for a resounding "yes" without hesitation. Regardless of their answer, you want to probe more deeply and ask "Why."

If you don't hear "yes" or "no" and see the question has made them a bit uncomfortable, you need to understand why. You can actually say,

"My question seems to have made you a bit uncomfortable, why is that?" Be prepared to hear things that aren't positive. No one is perfect. Know what you need from a manager to be successful. What others consider negative or even positive may not matter to you. You must balance the negative and the positive to make a well-informed decision.

What if you don't have anyone to speak to? Another place to look is LinkedIn and to figure out, as best you can, how many people have worked for this person and what kind of turnover there has been. Searching by the same title should yield the results you are seeking. If you look closely, you can guess how many people have been in the position you've been offered and how long they stayed. If you see more than one person leaving after six months, that is a red flag. The red flag is even more significant if multiple people have gone before six months. If numerous people leave after about a year, you must wonder why the tenure is so short.

You can also do a similar search by looking at the department. Search by "Company," "Past," and "Job Functions" to get an idea of what turnover looks like.

Another option is to check sites like Glassdoor. As stated previously, Glassdoor is an excellent place for disgruntled employees to bitch and moan, so you have to take what you read with a grain of salt. You are looking for the frequency of comments, the nature of the comments, and if there is an overriding theme across a variety of sources

Changing jobs isn't easy, and your relationship with your boss can determine whether the change is successful. It's essential to gather as much data as possible to be sure the person you will be working for is the person you think they are, and hopefully, more!

Key Messages

The relationship with your boss can determine your success or failure in a new role. When the relationship is strong, it will contribute greatly to your sense of satisfaction and accomplishment and growth. When it's not, it can be a challenge to difficult overcome.

Pay attention to your experience with your potential new boss during the hiring process. This is likely what you can expect if you say yes to an offer. If alarm bells start to go off pay attention. At least be aware of the tradeoffs if you say yes.

Do as much secondhand research as you can to calibrate what you see and hear during the interview. Pay attention to what people say and do when you ask them about the boss. How they respond is often more telling than what they say.

Coaching Questions

- What, if anything, have you missed in the past that you want to catch the next time?

- What do you need in a boss and how can you ask about that during the interview?

- What is your gut telling you?

CHAPTER 4: OFFER - Beware of Internal Equity

They Really Love Me—or Do They?

The scurry begins when you announce to your boss you are leaving. Your boss, your boss's boss, and HR try to find a way to get you to stay. While the attention may be flattering, and the specter of more money, responsibility, a flashy new title, or even a new stapler sounds enticing, don't forget the reason you started to look in the first place.

In most cases, money wasn't the reason you started to look. In a *Forbes* article titled "Beyond Money: The Real Reasons Employees Stay or Leave," Shep Hyken cited the Work Institute employee retention study conducted in 2022 that indicated the top five reasons employees leave

- No clear career path—this was true for almost 25% of the respondents
- Stress or lack of resources
- Health and family matters
- Work/life balance
- Money—about 1 in 10 leave because of money

A similar study reported by Jan Tegze in Recruiting Daily showed the top reason employees change jobs:

- Lack of opportunities to use skills and abilities—31%
- Bad management—22%

Searching For A Job Sucks!

- Toxic workplace/company culture—12%
- Promotion—8%
- Excessive work or too little of it—6%
- Higher salary and financial stability—6%
- Inadequate or lack of rewards and benefits—4%
- Other reasons—11%

As you can see, while money matters, it's not always the only reason people leave their jobs. So, think about it long and hard. Regardless of what you get promised, will your work change overnight? Will your boss suddenly become the best boss ever? Will the culture of your current organization change in one month, three months, six months, or even a year? I can confidently guarantee none of this will change, so while a counteroffer may sound tempting, don't kid yourself. The reasons you decided to leave will still be there, and it won't be long before you start looking for another job.

Research conducted by the software company Eclipse indicated that:

- About 80% of candidates who accept a counteroffer from their current employer end up leaving within six months.
- 9 out of 10 candidates who accept a counteroffer will leave their employer within 12 months.
- 50% of candidates who accept a counteroffer from their current employer will return to the job market after two

months—usually when the novelty of an increased salary and new responsibilities wears off

The lure of higher pay is a short-term solution to what is often a more complex problem. In many cases, it won't be long before you realize you are getting paid more to shovel the same you-know-what into the same bucket. What does that do for your career?

Besides, if you are that valuable to the organization, and a counteroffer proves that, do you want to work someplace where they knowingly paid you less than what you are worth because they could? On one hand, a counteroffer is flattering. Your value to the organization is validated and appreciated more than ever. On the other hand, this should make you angry. Think about it: Why are you finding out now, as you have one foot out the door, how valuable you are to the organization? Do you want to accept what amounts to a bribe to stay

So, What Can You Do?

Don't kid yourself and forget why you are receiving a counteroffer. A counteroffer is more about what's best for the company. Compared to having to recruit and hire a new employee, the disruption it creates when important work isn't completed, and the questions it creates for the employees left behind, a counteroffer is generally an inexpensive way to avoid disruption and a massive pain in the ass. Don't think for a single minute that a counteroffer is about you. Remind yourself again why you started to look in the first place

I understand that a new opportunity with many unknowns can be scary. Will you be successful? Will you like your boss? Will I like the people I work with? How will it affect those I love and care about? How long will it take to find the restroom? Changing jobs can be stressful, which is why many people stay put.

On the other hand, new opportunities give you a fresh start with the chance to learn, grow in your field, and make new connections. The right new opportunity is also how to build wealth, which is an important consideration. You are being hired because your future employer sees lots of potential, is willing to invest in your career, and is excited to make you part of the team. Do you see that same commitment where you currently work?

You also want to consider how the organization that made you the offer will react. They have likely spent much time and money to bring you on board. They have already started to make plans based on your anticipated start date. When you accept a counteroffer, realize that you may be burning a bridge and potentially damaging your professional reputation. You are severing relationships that may be difficult to recover. People take this personally and the people wh worked hard to bring you on board will never forget. They may lose their willingness to ever trust you again under any circumstances.

As reported by Redshift recruiting in a 2024 article titled "Why You Should Never Accept a Counteroffer": "In general, the risks of accepting a counteroffer are high and usually outweigh the rewards. You will miss out on all the opportunities associated with the new job and risk burning a bridge with your recruiter and prospective employer."

When you resign, be prepared to walk, and don't look back. By announcing your decision to leave, no one will ever forget that you are not quite as loyal as once thought. You can't honestly believe you will get that next promotion, prime assignment, or the biggest pay increase? Furthermore, if a counteroffer turns into a negotiation over salary, people will remember how you held the organization hostage. How much ill will is created, and what will the organization expect in return? Think very carefully before entertaining a counteroffer. Everything we know tells us they rarely work out.

Key Messages

Research shows us that accepting a counteroffer rarely works. Eventually, you realize that nothing is different and your reasons for wanting to leave in the first place haven't changed.

A counteroffer is less about you and more about what's best for the organization. It's easier to pay you more than spend lots of time, effort, and money to find someone to take your place.

Your organization will never forget you held them hostage. When you make your mind up to leave, leave. If you stay, your relationship with the organization will never be the same.

Coaching Questions

- How do you feel knowing you were underpaid and your organization knew it?

- How do you set expectations for what needs to change if you decide to stay?

- What were your reasons for leaving in the first place and do you honestly believe anything will change?

Searching For A Job Sucks!

Lessons from Job Seekers

There Is Always Something to Learn

Her entire career. she helps her clients think about how they can best attract, manage, and develop their talent. At times, she has been an individual contributor, and at other times she has led teams of people doing the work

Ellen made a job change about two and a half years ago when she thought the company that she was working for at the time was going to be sold to a larger company in the industry. At that time, her specialty area was a small part of the current company's overall mission, so she wasn't sure about the future given the potential sale. It was likely she would have to shift into another area of consulting which wasn't her passion or move into a management position and away from the work she loved.

While this disruption was occurring, a company that had reached out to her numerous times in the past, knocked on her door again and this time knocked harder with a strong financial offer that was too good to pass up. This appeared to be the opportunity to do the work she loved for a company that had lots of expertise in the areas she cared about. On the surface, it appeared to be a great fit. She had been with her current company a long time and didn't want to leave but saw this as her last hurrah and a chance to maximize her earning potential for the next five years and then possibly retire.

Unfortunately, her expectations of the new role were not a match with reality. Given the sign-on bonus the new company offered her when she joined the company, she would owe them a considerable

CHAPTER 4: OFFER - Beware of Internal Equity

amount of money were she to leave so she decided to stay put. She wasn't very happy, but she also wasn't miserable. The longer she stayed, she could feel the fun being sucked out of her work

She still had lots of friends at her former company that told leadership that, FYI, Ellen isn't very happy in her new company and if you want her back you can probably get her. They had always told Ellen the door was always open to return, but with the financial obligation to the new company, she thought it was impossible to leave. To her surprise, her former firm paid back what she owed the new company, and even though it didn't have an exact role for her to fill, it wanted her back. At that point, she was very happy to say "yes." Ultimately, Ellen believes if you will be happier and will enjoy the people you are working with more, and if the culture and values align better with who you are, it makes sense to put your pride or ego aside and go back.

One of the reasons Ellen was so happy to leave was because of a disconnect she saw in the culture. While they talked a lot about teamwork and collaboration, the rewards system and processes were much more about individual accomplishments and recognition. Ultimately, this is why this role was such a poor fit for Ellen.

What Ellen found most challenging was understanding how hard it is to start over once you are established at a place. When you are happy and decide to start over it is difficult. There were questions she should have asked and more due diligence she should have done to really understand how the new company operated and how they would set her up for success. Had she known more about the company, she would have realized it wasn't the best fit.

Searching For A Job Sucks!

Ellen emphasized that when you are looking at a new job, you want to interview companies as much as they want to interview you. You need to be sure it's what you want and need. In addition, people were not back in the office, so it was hard to make connections without meeting anyone

Her connections at her former company are what ultimately brought her back to it. Keeping up your network even after you leave is important. She also learned it is important to push back on an offer if it feels uncomfortable. Ellen agreed to a five-year promissory note, which is an extremely long clawback. She didn't worry about it at the time because things have always worked out for her, but in retrospect, she should have thought about it more. There was also a clause that would prevent her from working for a competitor for six months and the company would pay her salary during that time

For Ellen, culture really matters and having a good fit with who you are and what you value is incredibly important. This means you need to do your due diligence not only on the company, but also on the group that you will be joining. She would also say the grass is not always greener, and you need to decide on what matters most. For her, it was working with people whose values align with hers and where the culture treats people fairly. You need to find the best fit with how you like to work and what you need to be successful to make good decisions

Ellen believes there are a couple of ways you can figure out the culture. When interviewing, be sure you interview with all levels of the organization. What she learned after joining was that senior-level people were often treated differently; they get more respect and appreciation, and better benefits. People further down the org felt like second-class citizens. She could have asked questions like:

- How much say do you have on what projects you work on?

- What is your experience working with senior executives?

- Do you get lots of support and encouragement from senior executives?

- How is recognition given?

- Who receives recognition?

In retrospect, she didn't ask enough questions to pick up on things that might have been helpful to know. During the interview, Ellen couldn't get a firm answer on how bonuses were handled. She later learned it was not what they promised. They would decide when and how a bonus would be distributed and made sure employees would have to stay a few years to receive the full value of the bonus.

Looking back, except for the job she got right out of college, every job after that has been the result of knowing someone who helped open a door. She believes you can spread your networking too thin. It's not about the number of friends or followers you collect. She looks at her LinkedIn profile and is constantly amazed at some of the people and wonders how they got there because she doesn't even know who they are. It is also important to give back to help others. You never know how your paths may cross again.

Searching For A Job Sucks!

It's Okay to Say "No"

Mark is a 57-year-old Recruiting Manager who has worked in the recruiting industry his entire career. He describes his passion and expertise as helping companies transform how they recruit and hire talent.

Mark has had two jobs in the last four months. In the first case, he wasn't looking but was working in an industry that was going through a downturn with lots of upheavals. As a result, he was no longer able to influence positive outcomes, and the company was quickly moving into maintenance mode, which he didn't find very exciting.

Mark will admit he didn't do enough research on the first company he joined. Instead, he went to an industry that portrayed itself to be on a growth curve, and it absolutely wasn't.

The second jump was into an industry he is passionate about and is growing.

Mark considers himself very well networked. The first company he moved to was from a referral who recommended they talk to Mark. The second occurred when the person he worked for at the first company left and recruited him to join the second company.

Mark doesn't believe he has applied for a job since college. People he worked with in previous roles or knew him by reputation recruited him to new opportunities. His network of relationships introduced him to different and exciting opportunities.

CHAPTER 4: OFFER - Beware of Internal Equity

Based on all Mark has seen and personally experienced, he offers three pieces of advice to world-be job seekers. The first is to keep your network active and to leverage your network when you are looking for a job. Staying close to your network is how you get referred to others for possible opportunities. Mark strongly urges you to find a way to get referred. Find someone you know who might know someone at the company you want to join so you can get referred. This might be someone you know who has left the company you want to join, but probably still knows people who can help get your resume into the right hands. Use your network to get into an organization.

Referrals matter to hiring managers because they are often more trustworthy. Filling an open position is difficult and time-consuming. If someone makes a great referral, you have solved their problem. Mark knows hiring managers who will tell you that the person they interviewed for a job isn't who showed up for the job. Managers will trust people they know, so some form of endorsement will likely gain attention.

Mark has about 100 people he stays in touch with once a year. He is methodical about this and reaches out to people twice a week. He believes you need to be intentional about staying in touch, and focus less on collecting friends, connections, and followers. Certain people in his network know everybody. He reaches out to those people once a quarter because it is more of a relationship, even a friendship, than a connection.

Mark's second point has to do with the importance of research and learning about the company that might extend an offer. This is a lesson he learned the hard way. It is essential to understand the culture and how they are managed. Checking with Glassdoor and Indeed to provide reviews can be helpful, but in the same way, so are people in your network who work at that company and people they know who work or previously worked at that company. Look for people who can and will give you the straight skinny on an organization. Look for both confirming and disconfirming information and look for themes so you can form a clear picture of what to expect. After he left that company, a couple of people in his network commented afterward that they were surprised he went there. Had he asked them in advance, he would not have taken a role there.

And finally, his other advice is always to be running toward something, not away from something. He understands there are times when you hate your job and need to get out. His point is simple: if you aren't attracted to where you are going, you will likely make a bad decision, which he did.

He took his time before moving to his current company. He spoke with the CEO and asked questions about the vision for the company and the organization. For example, he asked the CEO what he had done wrong and would do over.

Mark's parting advice is perhaps the most powerful. Candidates need to understand it is okay to say "no." It's okay to say this isn't the right fit for me and walk away. The tendency is to think this is the only offer you will get, so you better say "yes." He sees people who don't critically assess the opportunity, the company, and leadership before deciding.

CHAPTER 4: OFFER - Beware of Internal Equity

Have a Plan

Karl is a 54-year-old executive who has been a COO and CEO for several well-known firms in the human capital industry. Karl's expertise is helping companies navigate difficult transitions. This could be setting up new sites, growth, restructuring, turnarounds, or reorganizations. He has honed these skills doing lots of work that others would prefer not to do because of all the inherent problems

Karl found himself looking for a new role when COVID crushed his last start-up. Karl looked for over two years before he found his next opportunity.

Karl saw the opportunity he was eventually offered posted on LinkedIn by a search firm with which he had a connection. He sent a note to a recruiter he knew at the search firm and asked for an introduction to the recruiter who had posted the job. After multiple interviews, he was hired.

The biggest challenge Karl faced during his search was staying motivated. He would review job boards and stay in touch with people he knew, but while he got close a couple of times, nothing materialized. It got to the point where he felt self-conscious about reaching out to the same people and wondered what they thought about him when they would see he was still looking. The day-to-day grind was exhausting and discouraging.

At one point in his search, Karl hired a company to help him with his resume and to send his resume to hundreds of companies and search firms. He thought the exposure would be helpful, but all he did was spend a lot of money for nothing in return. Updating his resume was frustrating because everyone has an opinion about how to put together a resume.

Karl was able to connect with lots of executive recruiters who would all say the same thing: they thought he was amazing, but they didn't have anything that was a good fit. Their advice was to keep doing what he was doing, and he would have something in a couple of months. Karl reached a point where he didn't know what to do, and this was hard for someone who solves difficult problems for a living. This was a problem he didn't know how to solve.

Upon reflection, Karl will tell you he never figured it out. He did acknowledge that he knows a lot of people and has a lot of connections because he has moved around so much, but not a lot of deep connections. Some of his deep connections had retired, which made the process more difficult.

Karl's greatest disappointment was that it took so long. He would see other people, whom he considered less capable, getting jobs and couldn't understand why he was having so much difficulty.

One of Karl's frustrations was the lack of follow-up by recruiters. He would speak with a recruiter who would promise to follow up, and 99% of the time never hear anything back. Even when the recruiter would give him something to do, they would never follow up.

What ultimately worked for Karl were job postings he found on LinkedIn where he could reach out directly. He would look for someone he knew who could make a warm introduction to the hiring manager or recruiter. Karl's words of wisdom are to "go direct." You may find the job on LinkedIn but avoid the applicant tracking system (ATS) black hole.

Karl learned the job search process sucks. He doesn't know if it is a process that can be documented or improved. He described it as a painful process with everyone having different advice and their own point of view. At times you feel like a ping pong ball going from one side of the net to another. Nothing seems to work, but when you are desperate you have to push yourself. You can find lots of coaches with lots of advice, but when you look at their backgrounds, they have never led or accomplished anything of significance except getting a coaching certificate.

Karl's advice: don't stop looking. You need to keep at it. Take a break when you need a break, but you can't stop. What kept him going was boredom and feeling like a failure and wanting to figure it out. Have a plan for each day so you can stay on task.

Searching For A Job Sucks!

CHAPTER 5: LANDING

You've Landed, but It Begins Again

You've said "yes," agreed on a start date, sent out all of the thank-you notes and can't wait to get started. After a long and tedious job search, there is no better feeling than finally landing. You are more than thrilled to put that job search folder away for a long time.

But wait. You aren't quite finished with your job search—not just yet. There is one last task to perform. And no recruiter or hiring manager is going to tell you or remind you. In fact, they kind of hope you forget. This is 100% on you and only in your best interest.

So, What Can You Do?

I'm guessing that during your search, there were friends, professional colleagues, former managers, and so on who helped you with your search. They may have made referrals, offered helpful advice and suggestions, provided recommendations, acted as a sounding board when you needed support, and made helpful introductions. One of them may have introduced you to someone, who introduced you to someone else, which led to an interview and an offer. These are the people who not only deserve a thank-you note, but that you want to stay in touch with for three reasons.

Searching For A Job Sucks!

First, reaching out every six months with an update on how you are doing in the new job is very much appreciated. If I have helped someone with their job search, it is gratifying to hear periodically how they are doing. It also validates what advice I give people is helpful and that feels great!

Second, if you are like most job seekers, whether your search was long or short, you were doing a lot of asking. Now is the time to do some "telling" and begin to pay it forward. Maybe you have expertise that would help someone solve a sticky problem, maybe you know something about the industry that someone would find useful, maybe you know people that would be good resources, maybe you know people looking for work who would be a good fit, and finally, maybe you can support someone who is struggling with their job search by serving as a sounding board and resource.

Third, it's very likely you will need their help and support again sometime in the future. By regularly staying in touch, it makes it much easier to ask for help.

Most people forget that networking is more about relationship-building, and there is no better way to build, maintain and nurture a relationship than by helping. My friend Kingsley Aikins, the CEO of the Networking Institute in Ireland, says "Networking is all about giving, not getting." Kingsley goes on to say that networking is how you can add value to your relationships by putting your network at the disposal of other people.

I refer to this close group of connections you stay in touch with as "My Vital Few"™ and it's more important than ever after you land. All of us have the tendency to put our heads down and go to work.

CHAPTER 5: LANDING - You've Landed, but It Begins Again

Before you know it, weeks, months, or even years have passed, and these once most valuable relationships begin to fade.

Why this matters, relates to the third reason why these connections are so critical to your career. I know from experience and from research that staying in close contact with these most critical relationships is how you hear about new opportunities you don't know exist. Many of the most talented people I know, rarely, if ever have to look for a job. The jobs find them. How? By staying in close contact with people who know you, know what you are good at, and know what you like to do. You want your network to have you in mind 24/7/365 so when they hear about something that sounds interesting, you are the first person they call. If you know those people who land in amazing new opportunities without looking, this is how they do it. Set a goal that you will never have to search for a job again. You can do it, but you can't wait until you are unhappy or unemployed.

If for some reason you have to start a search, these are the people, your My Vital Few™, you will reach out to first for assistance. It's uncomfortable to call or email someone you haven't spoken to in months or years asking for help. Maybe you've received one of those awkward emails or calls from someone. I knw I have, and I know immediately why they are reaching out to me. Don't put yourself in a position where you have to send that awkward email or make the awkward call. Keeping in touch with people at some regular interval is easy if you commit to putting in the effort. From what I have observed working with thousands of highly capable professionals, it may be the most important time you invest in your career.

Searching For A Job Sucks!

Key Messages

Once most people find a new job, the tendency is to forget about their job search and move forward. In fact, if you never want to search for a job again, once you land triggers the My Vital Few™ process. This is the time to identify those people who were the most help with your search and build a plan to regularly stay in touch with them.

The other reason you engage the My Vital Few™ process. is to pay it forward. Regularly reaching out and asking how you can help is the best way to build, nurture, and maintain those most important relationships.

Coaching Question

- Who helped you the most with your job search and who do you consider part of your My Vital Few™?

- How do you plan to keep organized so you reach out regularly?

- What expertise or knowledge do you have that you can share with others?

CHAPTER 5: LANDING - You've Landed, but It Begins Again

Lessons from Job Seekers

Most People Want to Help—Karma Is a Boomerang

Bob is 48 years old and for the past 20-plus years, has been in the digital advertising industry. During that time, he led digital sales teams for some well-known brands. Bob is a very accomplished executive who found himself at the short end of downsizing when the company he was working for needed to cut costs quickly

Bob was offered two opportunities within a month, but they weren't right. Bob looked for about two months before finding a new job. Bob is used to being busy 24 hours a day, 7 days a week, and coming to a complete stop was hard for him.

What Bob found most challenging about his search was talking to companies about roles where he thought he was highly qualified and getting to the ninth inning and having it not work out. There were two opportunities where there was lots of mixed communication from the client, company, or recruitment firm. He was working with a contingent search firm on one of the opportunities. The other was from a friend who made a referral.

Bob always talks to recruiters when they reach out, so he could call on that network when he started his search.

Without a doubt, Bob believes his network is the key to finding a new job.

A good friend, the CRO of another organization, put him in touch with the person he described as the best recruiter in the business, and this led to a new opportunity.

Searching For A Job Sucks!

When he was initially laid off, many of his friends said to take some time off and retrench and regroup with family and friends and try not to jump right back into the fray. He didn't do that and was very aggressive with his search and was talking to people from day one. Looking back, he wished he had the ability to stop and relish the time a bit.

While he might have paused more, Bob says there is very little he would have done differently. He has been working most of his life, so being unemployed felt unnatural, and it was hard not to be restless.

Regarding advice, Bob believes more people are willing to be helpful than you realize. When people he doesn't know reach out to him over LinkedIn with a specific ask, he is always happy to help.

If someone approaches him with a general request such as, "I'd like to pick your brain on something," he won't respond. But if someone says "Hi, Bob, you've been in digital advertising for 20 years, and I'd love to know what a new graduate like me needs to do to break into the industry," he is happy to respond and be helpful. From Bob's perspective, why be a jerk? Karma is a boomerang.

Bob acknowledges that rejection is hard and is often part of the process. He reflected on a quote, saying that if you are breathing in this world, you have a purpose. It's easy to get discouraged, but as his father used to say, it only takes one call, one conversation, and one open door. Think about the positives in life. Recall when you have been discouraged, how you got yourself through tough times, and that you can do it again. Being out of work can be difficult on several levels—mentally, physically, and financially—but you've faced challenges before and will get through this too. You just need to keep pushing forward.

Be Kind to Yourself

Sally is 41 years old and a Vice President of Government Affairs for a small firm, reporting to the CEO. Prior to this, she was a government relations/communications individual contributor for one of the world's largest oil and gas firms. Sally has worked in government relations almost her entire career.

Sally had been looking for a new job for a while because she wanted to grow professionally, and she didn't see opportunities to take on new challenges at her previous company. The position she found is amazing and she is thrilled she made the change.

Sally has learned that you never burn bridges. She remains in contact with former colleagues because, if you like the company, leadership will change, and you may have the option to return in a different position.

Sally started to look more earnestly when she started to be recruited and realized she was being considered for more senior-level roles. The hardest part was getting to the final round and not getting the offer. That happened to her four times. After you have invested so much time, you start to envision yourself in a new role and not getting an offer is devastating. Sally took some time off from job searching to take time to recover. It's like dating: after a big rejection, you need some time off.

Searching For A Job Sucks!

Sally also found it annoying to upload a resume and then type in the same information. She would stop applying for a job when the process was so frustrating.

The worst part about being a finalist and not getting an offer was how she found out. Two of the four companies where she had been a finalist sent a form letter telling her she didn't get the job. In one case, this was after six rounds of interviews and being flown to HQ and meeting with the CEO. This was a consumer-facing company, and it lost a customer in the process because she was so frustrated by the way she was treated. She expected much more of a human touch. She has also had instances where she went for an interview and never heard anything. She was completely ghosted and couldn't believe the lack of consideration.

She found her current job posted on LinkedIn. After she applied, she found out that a woman she knows who also works in government relations had been engaged to help review resumes. When this woman saw Sally's resume, she immediately flagged it and said to the hiring team they needed to talk to her.

Sally was able to get several interviews and what worked for her was doing the necessary research to make it a great conversation. She reviewed the website, looked at the social media of everyone who would interview her, read press releases and listened to earnings calls, and read the CEOs tweets to ensure she was fully prepared.

Sally was able to demonstrate her preparation artfully during the interview by referencing the mission or the most recent news and how it would impact this role. She would connect it to how she could add value. This is how doing the research can lead to a positive impression.

If she knew someone at the company where she had applied, she would ask them to flag her resume and put it in front of the hiring manager. She would also reach out to people she knew who might know someone to see if they could help.

What she learned going through the process was increased humility. We each have a brand and not everyone will want what you offer. All you can do is be yourself. You can't portray yourself as someone you aren't. You don't want to accept an offer and find out later it isn't a good fit.

The other lesson here is to look for a job when you have a job. This helps you avoid feeling desperate, which is often a red flag for employers.

Sally believes one of the biggest challenges is figuring out what the organization's culture is really like. In her profession, everyone knows everyone so she can find people who can give her the straight scoop. Glassdoor might give you some context, but no one goes to Glassdoor to say great things about where they work. You need to take it with a grain of salt. If you think of culture as an iceberg, you need to understand what exists below the waterline.

As Sally reflects on her job search experience, and if she had to do it over, she would have been kinder to herself. This is a very personal process and many of us show compassion to our friends during their ups and downs, but we don't show the same grace to ourselves.

Searching For A Job Sucks!

When you get a rejection letter it hurts. No one wants to be rejected. Do what will make you feel good, something that will remind you of your value. Talk to friends, listen to music, but ultimately, you must remember your value. This is a humbling, challenging process that can take the wind out of your sails. Rejection will ultimately wear on anyone. You have to hang in and keep doing the work. It will eventually pay off.

In one case, because of some personal outreach and connections, Sally was offered a job very quickly, but she didn't know about salary or benefits until they sent her an offer letter. Had it not gone so quickly she would have had the conversation about compensation sooner, but ultimately, she couldn't take such a pay cut. She prefers to know information about compensation upfront so she doesn't waste anyone's time, including her own.

Sally's advice is to use your direct connections and reach out to your secondary level of connections as well.

Sally also believes it is important to follow up with people when someone says "Please follow up" She believes that only 30% of the people follow up. When you are early in your career, you doubt if someone really means it, you don't know what to say you feel self-conscious, and you don't want to waste anyone's time; she regrets not doing that earlier in her career.

Sally shares a great example of this when she was early in her career and met a senior-level woman who was amazing. The woman gave Sally her card and asked her to follow up. For all of the reasons just mentioned, Sally talked herself out of following up. Years later, she reached out with the following note:

In a million years, you would never remember me. I moved to DC for grad school at American in 2004, and you and I met at one of my first networking events. You were kind enough to give me your card and said I should follow up with you. I never did because I was terrified of DC and didn't think you'd ever write back anyway. By the time I found the moxie, I'd lost your card. All these years later, I share that story when I meet young women looking for advice or help connecting. I tell them not to miss out on opportunities, that they will regret it, that they shouldn't be afraid to follow up with anyone. So thank you for inspiring that in me, even though I missed the opportunity to connect when I was young and new to the city. :)

She heard back and the woman was lovely. It may be harder when you are a 25-year-old professional, but the lesson here is simple: when people offer, step into the offer, and see where it leads.

Sally is also having lunch next week with her former boss at the company she left. Her boss was sad to see her leave, but excited to see a woman take on a leadership role, and Sally is committed to staying in touch with her.

Sally talks with her friends about career strategy and where she wants to be 5, 10, 15 years out. She wants to know what she should be doing now to move her toward those objectives. It is very easy to get attracted to the next shiny object when a recruiter calls with what is always an "amazing opportunity." You need to step back and ask how it fits with the larger plan you have for yourself. Is the opportunity a new experience that offers the chance to learn more and grow or will you be doing the same job over in a new organization? You must ask yourself if a move like that makes sense.

Searching For A Job Sucks!

Never Burn Bridges

Barry is a 55-year-old change management executive. He describes himself as a transformation executive. He has been a marketing, product, strategy, technology, and operations executive, and in each case, his mission was to drive change and significant improvement.

After finishing his more recent transformation assignment, Barry was ready for his next opportunity. He looked for about 10 months before landing his new role

What he found most challenging during his search was a reality in the consulting world he didn't know. After looking for a couple of months and having multiple interviews and great conversations with several different firms, he didn't understand why no one was making an offer. This was until a close colleague pulled him aside and told him that none of the well-known consulting firms would hire someone over 50 years old for a senior role. This was an industry secret that cost him two months. In one case, he had 15 interviews before hearing the firm was going in another direction. All the other opportunities gradually disappeared.

What he found most frustrating was how long the hiring process takes. When he is on the hiring side, he thinks he is going super-fast. When he is a candidate, it seems like the process moves super-slowly.

In one instance, a very senior contact never followed through, which was disappointing. He expected more and it didn't materialize. In another case, a close contact referred him to the right people that led to his new opportunity. People always say don't burn bridges and have a strong network, and it couldn't be truer. Barry doesn't expect his network to find him a role, but when he finds something, he taps into them as a reference.

Barry saw this new role posted and reached out to an executive at the company who he had worked with in the past. He mentioned the role, and they had a conversation. After he applied, he learned the hiring manager was connected to another executive from his last position. This person shot a note to the hiring manager who also recommended him for the role. Barry had two recommendations from two highly regarded executives that bumped his resume to the top of the pile.

As part of the interviewing process, a consultant from one of the big firms was part of the process and knew of Barry's reputation. This person also recommended Barry to the hiring manager. In the end, before Barry ever met with the hiring manager, he had been recommended by three people. This was a role for him to lose. Having a good reputation and never burning bridges is how you use your network. You want to make it easy for people to help but you can't rely on other people to find you a job. That's the heavy lifting only you can do.

If he had to do it over, even though he loved his last opportunity, he has now learned that taking calls and listening to other opportunities is smart. He let his networking activity take a back burner because he never planned to leave. One organization change, one change in leadership, one hard market, and the whole world changes. Some days you find yourself on the wrong side of the fence even though you don't know how you got there.

Searching For A Job Sucks!

Barry's advice is to stay calm during the job search process. Think through what you enjoy and put together your own personal values statement. He made sure that when he was searching and looking, he stayed true to what he likes and enjoys. This made it easy to talk about what he loves during the interview.

He shared that he almost did the wrong thing. There was a role locally and the compensation and the role were a fraction of his current scope. He hit it off with the hiring manager, but told her he wasn't interested. After a few months of looking, probably because he was feeling desperate, he went back to the hiring manager and had a conversation. She was the one who said he was way too qualified for the role and encouraged him to stay with the search.

The lesson here is to embrace the discomfort and stay with the pain as long as you can until you find the right opportunity. When you don't and you settle, it isn't long before you find yourself looking again.

Never Assume a Job Is Forever

Sam is 60 years old and has been a manager or director in Human Resources for most of his career. In his current role he is a contractor.

Sam's expertise is in human resources development. He's done everything from talent management to performance management, employee engagement, organization development, and learning and development.

Sam was looking because he realized quickly in his last role that it wasn't going to work. The vice president who hired Sam wanted to transform talent management and succession. The company wanted to dramatically shift its industry focus and the VP convinced Sam that Talent Management was going to be more imperative and help lead the charge. It turns out the company wasn't ready for that journey, and within months, the VP who hired Sam was let go. It wasn't long before the resources dedicated to this initiative started to dwindle, and Sam realized he needed to look for a job.

Sam found his new role through a personal connection. He started looking in October and landed in April. He worked his network and applied for appropriate roles. He had plenty of interviews and the process for his current role moved quickly. As it turns out, there wasn't an actual job when Sam first engaged with the company. Sam was connected to a manager who had a need tied to an existing project, but it wasn't well defined. Over two months of conversations and based on how the larger project was proceeding and the required skills, Sam and the manager collaborated on a position description that made sense.

Sam's search was about six months. He was working his full-time job while keeping his eyes open for new opportunities.

Sam has been in a job search mode a couple of times in his career and not knowing where and when the search will end is the most challenging.

He had interviews in February that went so well the company was talking to Sam as if he was already in the job. Then suddenly the phone stopped ringing and when he called, nobody returned his calls, and this was after talking about starting as soon as the following Monday!

Searching For A Job Sucks!

The stop-and-start aspect of the job search is what he finds most difficult. Unlike some people, Sam finds he has lots of energy for a job search. He enjoys networking and the exertion of effort to find a job. The job of finding a job requires its own skill set and he enjoys meeting people, shaking hands, talking to people, understanding their perspective, and discovering where there might be a fit. That process gives him energy.

What makes the job search hard is not knowing when it will end. It's the unknown that creates anxiety and fuels a relentless commitment to keep pounding away. Sam knows people who have worked hard to find a new job and never took a break between the old role and the new. Afterward they kicked themselves for not taking more time for themselves. The fear of missing out (FOMO) is powerful.

Sam believes the right job will eventually step forward, and if one he is genuinely passionate about doesn't materialize, it simply wasn't meant to be. He learned long ago to stop beating his head against the wall when an interview doesn't work out. He views it as fate's way of navigating you to the right opportunity.

Sam will tell you there are peaks and valleys in the job search. You either have nothing for a couple of months and you are in the pits of despair, or when you are about to get an offer from one company, three others show up and you must decide the right criteria to choose the best option.

Sam's belief and fervent advice is to never assume a job is forever. You need the mentality that every job is short to medium term, and you always need to be networking. Never put your bags down and rest.

He also knows some people find the thought of perpetual networking exhausting. His advice is to focus on a smaller group of critical friends and colleagues you count on when you need them.

Always be open and start conversations with the idea that you could be looking for a job a year from now. This will help you from being devastated when the company says it isn't working, or in his case, the role completely unravels. You just can't completely unplug from the idea of looking for a job, so you don't get caught off guard when a company changes its mind about their priorities.

The big pivot for Sam was taking a role that has a time limit attached to it. He has spent his entire career as an "employee" or W-2, and while he likes the current opportunity, he had to shift his thinking and get his head around a contract or 1099. This job is also remote, which five years ago would never have been on the table. It is important to be open to new and different ways of working.

When he thinks back to his last opportunity and the interviewing process, he realizes it is easy to torture yourself for not asking the right questions to really understand the company psyche. As soon as you think you have the right questions, you will inevitably miss the one that uncovers what lies beneath the waterline and shows you most what you need to know to make a good decision. Companies are reticent to share what job seekers most need to uncover. And even when an interviewer is honest and dumps all the dirty little secrets on the table, you don't always have enough context or the capacity to hear it fully to understand what they are really saying. Or you think you are the savior who can fix everything, and you miss an important point.

Searching For A Job Sucks!

Sam's advice is to not put 150% into any one job or give your soul to the company as it will never be reciprocated. The way people complain about millennials is the perfect response to today's environment. Millennials don't get too involved with one company. They see themselves in a profession as opposed to a job. As soon as they don't see themselves learning and developing, doing interesting work, being entertained, and being paid correctly, they move onto the next thing. People might complain, but you can't expect anything more given corporate behavior. Don't over-invest in a company and burn yourself out trying to solve every problem. Live life, be balanced, develop yourself, and continually assess if what you have is working.

CHAPTER 6:
PUTTING IT ALTOGETHER

The Job Search Game Plan

Whenever I was faced with a major project, my friend and former colleague Dan Gillick was famous for asking "What's the game plan?" That was Dan's way of ensuring we achieved a level of detail and organization required to execute, and ultimately, ensure success. It was the right question to ask and led to many useful conversations and exciting outcomes.

The same is true for a job search. All of the strategies, advice, wisdom, and tactics shared in this book or anywhere else are only useful if you have a game plan to execute. What I often see are haphazard approaches with job seekers grasping for anything that might work. The most successful approach is to have a clear and organized plan that guides how you spend your time and resources.

The Job Search Game Plan consists of 10 steps spread out over the course of a week.

1. Preparing

2. Following up

3. Searching job boards

Searching For A Job Sucks!

4. Reaching out to your *A*-level connections

5. Reaching out to your *B*- and *C*-level connections

6. Reaching out to search firms

7. Reaching out to alumni

8. Reaching out to companies where you would like to work

9. Interviewing and receiving an offer

10. Landing

If you are engaged in a job search, it is important to know what you are doing every day of the week. You never want a day when you wake up and have no idea how to spend your time. Searching for a job can be challenging, frustrating, and lonely. Without a plan, it is easy to throw up your hands and give up. While you know you can't quit, it is easy to become paralyzed with indecision about what to do next. To avoid that happening, you need a weekly game plan to stay focused and on track. View this as a repeatable process that, if executed well, can lead to amazing success. My advice is to stick with the plan, learn along the way, and adjust based on what you are learning.

Preparing

The process starts with the preparation phase that is covered earlier in the book. The book was organized this way, so you know where and how to start. I know the temptation for many is to jump in and immediately start applying for jobs. Knowing that you often only get one bite at the apple, it's important to be completely ready when you take that one shot. My advice, go slow up front so you can go faster later. Don't race past the preparation step. The work in this first step lays the foundation for everything that follows.

Monday

If you are doing the networking part of your job search well, on Monday morning when you sit down at your desk, you will have a list of 5 to 15 people whom you need to contact this week. These are people you need to follow up with to provide an update, call or schedule with, or friends who can provide emotional support.

While this first step may seem out of place, it's a reminder of the work you need to be doing if you expect to find a new opportunity sooner rather than later. Having this list of people to contact is based on your work in the previous weeks. If this isn't your experience, you need to work harder at this aspect of your search.

To keep track of this activity, you can create a task in Outlook or put events directly on your calendar. Better yet, I have created a Networking Guide and Tracking tool that is available for job seekers on my website https://fitzdrakesearch.com.

Following Up

As you already know, following up with your networking connections at a regular internal is the key to a successful networking effort.

Here is a sample follow up email.

Subject: Follow up from Michael Scott

Searching For A Job Sucks!

Hi, Susan,

Good morning. I hope you are having a good week.

As promised, I'm happy to provide you with an update to my job search. Over the past few weeks, I have had 4 interviews. One role didn't work out and the other 3 at ABC, XYZ and QRS companies are still active.

I truly appreciate the support and advice you have provided. Your assistance during this process has been invaluable.

If you think of anyone else that could provide advice or insight, I would sincerely appreciate the referral. The more people I meet increases the odds of finding that right opportunity. If I've learned anything in this process, it's all about relationships.

I am learning a lot about the job market and how different companies operate, if that would help with any of your recruiting. I am happy to share what I know.

Thank you again for your support and I look forward to following up.

Cheers,

Michael

You obviously need to personalize this draft, so it fits your style and the relationship with your networking contact.

Here is another example to consider:

Subject: Follow up from Jeffrey Lebowski

CHAPTER 6: PUTTING IT ALTOGETHER - The Job Search Game Plan

Hi, Walter,

Good morning. I hope your week is going well. Thank you again for all of your assistance with my job search. Your support and guidance are greatly appreciated.

I've made progress in the last 2 months having interviewed with 4 different companies—ABC, XYZ, QRS and TUV. All 4 have invited me back for a second interview so I'm excited to see some progress. I am probably most interested in QRS as I connected exceptionally well with the person who would be my boss.

As I continue down this path, I am open to any additional referrals or recommendations you can share. I am learning this is all about relationships, so I am happy to meet as many people as possible.

I am learning a lot about the job market and how different companies operate, if that would help with any of your recruiting. I am happy to share what I know.

Thank you again for your support and I look forward to following up.

Cheers,

Jeffrey

Not following up is where many job seekers fall short. In my experience, job seekers don't follow up at all or follow up only once. When someone gives you permission to follow up, by agreeing to receive follow ups or by responding to your follow ups, don't stop. This is a relationship you want to cultivate and maintain long after you have landed. Many job seekers feel embarrassed to continually

Searching For A Job Sucks!

follow up with nothing to show. First of all, you do have something to show, and you do have something to share. Second, don't worry what the recipient might be thinking when they receive your email. They understand the process and know it is hard. There is a good chance they have been in your shoes at some point in their career.

Searching Job Boards

Once you complete your follow ups, consider the rest of Monday as job board day. Regardless of the board, review each one and see what might be new. Hopefully you have set alerts, so you hear when something interesting is posted. Regardless, you'll want to jump in and see what's new. You also never know what you might have missed. There is peace of mind knowing you are aware of the posted opportunities.

It doesn't hurt to repeat that one key to using job boards successfully is to thoughtfully apply to jobs that make sense. Customize your resume accordingly and do the work that is described earlier in the book so you can slide in the back door. Going in the back door increases your odds of getting called, and it's also a way to further build out your network.

You'll want to create an application and interview tracker that is separate from your networking effort so you can follow up as necessary.

Sample back door letter:

Subject: Manager of Digital Marketing Opportunity

Dear Mike,

I am writing to apply for the Manager of Digital Marketing opportunity I see posted on your company website. Job posting 12321. I have a well-rounded background in Digital Marketing, and I am excited about joining ABC.

My accomplishments include:

- *Successfully launched a digital marketing campaign that resulted in a 15% increase in brand visibility and engagement*

- *Implemented marketing strategies that led to a 12% increase in customer acquisition and retention*

- *Managed a cross-functional marketing team that delivered 5 projects on time and within budget*

- *Executed successful digital marketing initiatives, such as SEO optimization, social media campaigns, and email marketing that increased traffic by 20% and increased conversions by 35%*

I look forward to speaking with you and learning more about your specific challenges.

Sincerely,

Susan Smith

Here is another example of a backdoor letter:

Subject: Director of Operations at ABC

Dear Walter,

Searching For A Job Sucks!

I am writing to apply for the Director of Operations role I saw posted on your company website. Posting #739218.

My background includes a long track record of success in large and small companies, maximizing operational and financial efficiency.

Examples of my accomplishments include:

- *Increased operational efficiency by 22%, resulting in a cost savings of over $2M achieved through process improvements*

- *Reduced production lead times by 10% and increased on-time delivery by 28%*

- *Increased profit margin by 8% as the result of operational improvements*

- *Improved net promoter scores (NPS) by 14% as the result of operational enhancements*

I would like to learn more about the challenges facing (name of company) and discuss how I can contribute to your success. I look forward to speaking at your convenience.

Sincerely,

Donny Kerabatsos

Both of these emails are short and focus heavily on accomplishments. Don't waste time trying to convince someone you are a team player with lots of energy. You'll hopefully get the opportunity to do that later in the process. For now, I give you the benefit of the doubt that you have the technical and functional chops to do the job.

Of late, I find myself recommending an even shorter email and embedding my resume directly into the email. I start the email with the best statement I can to generate attention and draw their eyes to my easy-to-read resume. Here is an example:

Subject: Director of Operations at ABC

Dear Walter,

I have 15 years of experience as an operations executive at XYZ company and ABC company and have increased operational efficiency by 22% and achieved $2M in cost savings.

I am very interested in your Director of Operations role – posting #739218 and have included my resume below.

Sincerely,

Donny Kerabatsos

Here is why I like this approach – people don't read, they glaze. If I can quickly glaze and see something that gets my attention, my eyes will be drawn the to the resume that has been copied and pasted into the resume. Remember, at this point in the process your objective isn't to get a call, your objective is to be seen.

There is no such thing as one size fits all. You want to customize these emails as much as possible and wherever possible. If someone who knows the recipient referred you, mention their name in the

Searching For A Job Sucks!

subject line. If you work for a well-known, highly regarded organization, mention that upfront.

While there are general boards like LinkedIn, there are many niche job boards, too numerous to mention, based on your industry and or functional area of expertise. These are often better than general job boards and where available, preferred by recruiters. Recruiters often think of job boards as a necessary evil and often a waste of time but the candidate quality on niche boards is generally considered to be higher and more on target.

Applying to jobs you find on job boards is a passive job search strategy. It is necessary, but not sufficient. Once you complete your passive job board work each week, it's time to engage an active job search strategy. An active search consists of several components and is where you will spend the rest of your week and the majority of your time—when you aren't interviewing or preparing to interview.

Another way to find jobs, and I am surprised at how many people don't do this, is to use Google. Use the Google search engine and type in the job title you seek plus the word jobs, and you will be surprised by the number of opportunities that get returned. You can even add the name of a city after jobs if you want to focus on a specific geography. For example, "CTO jobs Boston." I'll warn you in advance, your Google search may return lots of options, but it is worth the time to scroll through them. While you may have seen some of these jobs other places like on LinkedIn, for example, you will also find jobs that are listed on niche job boards, company career web pages, and other places you may forget to look or may not even know about.

Tuesday to Thursday— Let the Networking Begin

Reaching Out to A-Level Connections—Your My Vital Few™

Your *A*-level connections are the first people you call when you need support, assistance, or advice and they hold you in the same regard. As I've stated earlier in the book, you aren't asking for a job. It's about engaging in conversation and learning what you can to help your search.

Subject: Following up and seeking your advice

Hi, Chris,

I hope this message finds you well and that your week is off to a great start.

I wanted to touch base and follow up on our conversation from four months ago. Since then, I've been contemplating my next career move, and I've come to the decision to explore new opportunities. Your insights and guidance have always been invaluable, and I believe your perspective will be incredibly beneficial to me as I navigate this transition.

Would you be available to connect and share your thoughts on my job search strategy? I'm eager to brainstorm potential opportunities and gather your feedback on my approach. Additionally, I was hoping you might be able to offer recommendations for individuals or resources that have a solid grasp of the current job market landscape. Do you happen to know any reputable recruiters whom you could suggest?

Searching For A Job Sucks!

I have several questions and topics I'd like to discuss with you, and I'm flexible with scheduling. Please let me know some days and times that work for you, and I'll do my best to work around your schedule.

Thank you in advance for your time and assistance. I truly appreciate your support as I embark on this journey.

Warm regards,

Bill

Here is another letter with a different context:

Subject: Following up and seeking your advice

Hi, Mary.

I trust this message finds you well.

I want to share with you that I've recently parted ways with Joe's Rag Shop. Unfortunately, due to a slowdown in the business, they made the difficult decision to downsize, resulting in a reduction of 15% of the workforce, myself included along with others in our department.

I'm reaching out to see if we could arrange a time to connect either by phone or in person. I value your insights and was hoping to seek your feedback on my job-search strategy and engage in some brainstorming together. Additionally, I'm curious if you might be able to introduce me to someone knowledgeable about the current job market trends and where to focus my search. Moreover, I'd *greatly appreciate any recommendations you might have for reputable recruiters in the field.*

I have a few questions that I believe your experience could help with and would be grateful for your guidance.

Please let me know your availability, and I'll do my best to accommodate your schedule.

Thank you for your time and consideration.

Best,

Dan

Unfortunately, we aren't always great at keeping up with our closest connections. As I've heard from many, life just gets in the way. Here is another letter with a different context that might come in handy. While the body of the letter looks the same as others, the introduction makes a connection that will hopefully be well received.

Subject: Hi from Scott Bartle

It's great to reconnect with you after such a long time! Please accept my apologies for not staying in touch more regularly.

I want to share with you that I've made the decision to explore new career opportunities. While my time at Gadgets has been incredibly rewarding, I believe it's time to seek out a fresh challenge.

Would you be available to schedule a time for us to chat and brainstorm about my job-search strategy? Additionally, I'm curious if you might know of anyone who could provide insights into the current job market landscape and where I should focus my energies. Furthermore, I'd greatly appreciate any recommendations you might have for respected recruiters in the industry.

I have a few questions that I believe your expertise could help answer, and I would value your insight greatly.

Please let me know your availability, and I'll do my best to accommodate your schedule.

Looking forward to catching up.

Pat

I won't repeat it here, but the strategy for reaching out when you don't hear back from people is covered in my first book. *How to Find a New Job Without Looking* provides the templates messaging and strategy for conducting a rigorous networking effort that ultimately achieves results.

Reaching Out to Your B- and C-Level Connections

Your *B*-level connections are people you know or know reasonably well. Your *C*-level connections are exactly that: connections. You don't know them at all or very little.

The email is very similar to the preceding ones with a different introduction. This is an example of an email to send when you haven't been in touch with someone for a long time. The body of the letter is the same, but the introduction is welcoming and hopefully generates a response.

Subject: Hi from Joe Smith

CHAPTER 6: PUTTING IT ALTOGETHER - The Job Search Game Plan

Hi Barbara—

I hope this finds you well. I know we haven't connected in quite some time. Please accept my apologies for not doing a better job of staying in touch.

I want to share with you that I've made the decision to explore new career opportunities. While my time at Gadgets has been incredibly rewarding, I believe it's time to seek out a fresh challenge.

Would you be available to schedule a time for us to chat and brainstorm about my job-search strategy? Additionally, I'm curious if you might know of anyone who could provide insights into the current job market landscape and where I should focus my energies. Furthermore, I'd greatly appreciate any recommendations you might have for respected recruiters in the industry.

I have a few questions that I believe your expertise could help answer, and I would value your insight greatly.

Please let me know your availability, and I'll do my best to accommodate your schedule.

Looking forward to catching up.

Joe

Another way to start this email could be with the following:

Hi Barbara—

I trust this message finds you well and keeping busy. It's been a while since we last connected, and I wanted to take a moment to reach out. I apologize for not making more of an effort to stay in touch.

The general idea is to soften up the introduction when you've been out of touch with someone for a while.

The other letter is when you don't know someone that well but would still like to engage their support.

Hi, Barbara—

I hope this message finds you well. I'm happy to reconnect with you after our previous conversation, despite the lapse in time since our last interaction. My schedule has been quite hectic the last 6 months, and unfortunately, I've fallen behind in keeping in touch.

Reaching Out to Search Firms

Reaching out to search firms is covered earlier in the book. The best way to connect with a search firm is with a warm introduction from a referral. You can also reach out on your own, but the odds of making a live connection are much lower. When you make one of these connections, never let it go!

Here is an example of how to contact a search firm when you have a referral.

Subject: Referral from Bob Fitz

Hello Dan,

I'm pleased to virtually meet you. Bob Fitz, the Vice President of Sales from Joe's Rag Shop whom you previously worked with,

CHAPTER 6: PUTTING IT ALTOGETHER - The Job Search Game Plan

recommended I get in touch. From what I gather, you specialize in placing operations leaders and general management executives within leading Fortune 1000 corporations.

With a solid background spanning two decades in global business operations, I have the ability to manage multiple divisions and sites, business process outsourcing, contract negotiations, vendor relationships, significant project and program oversight, along with strategic alliance building. Throughout my career, I've successfully managed operations worth over $1B and led international teams exceeding 10,000 members. Moreover, I played a pivotal role in the integration processes during our company's most significant merger.

At this juncture, I'm open to exploring executive opportunities at the COO or CEO level. Bob thought you would be a good person for me to contact.

I'm also happy to share insights into the evolving landscapes of the Financial Services and Human Capital sectors, which are both expanding and undergoing considerable transformations.

I am looking forward to arranging a conversation at your earliest convenience. I'll make sure to accommodate your schedule to the best of my ability.

Best wishes,

Liza

You will note that the name of the person making the referral is front and center. This is your best chance of getting noticed. There is nothing better than a warm introduction.

Searching For A Job Sucks!

Here is another version that doesn't rely on a warm introduction. The note is short, so hopefully they take a quick look at your resume. The goal is for your resume to be placed in their data base so other members of the firm can find it.

Subject: VP of Sales looking to connect

Hi Dan,

I am currently or (most recently I was) the VP of Sales at Joe's Rag Shop and I am looking to make a change. If you are looking for an Operations VP or COO who can manage multiple divisions and sites, business process outsourcing, contract negotiations, vendor relationships, significant project, and program oversight, along with strategic alliance building I would love to speak.

I am also happy to introduce you to people in my network for other active searches you may have.

My resume is attached.

Bob

Here is another version that is a little longer with more detail.

Subject: COO looking to connect

Hi, Marty,

Good morning.

My name is Jeff Labowski, and I am the COO of XYZ, a $100M professional services and advisory firm with multiple service offerings and 500 employees.

I've been with XYZ for over a year now and things are going well. We are making several strategic acquisitions to grow our business that have been exciting. I'm leading changes throughout the

firm for a more efficient, scalable business model to increase our growth and to improve our financials.

My goal is to be the CEO of a mid-sized organization. Should you see a CEO opportunity that looks like a good fit, please let me know.

I look forward to staying in touch. If you have any open roles where access to my network would be helpful, let me know. I am happy to make an introduction.

Thanks,

Jeff

If your email is remotely close to what a recruiter cares about, they will take a quick look and share it with their colleagues. You only need to connect with one person at a search firm to be included in its database—assuming they see some potential. There is the slight chance someone will reach out to you in the future if they see a match. It's a long shot, but you never know when it might pay off.

Searching For A Job Sucks!

Reach Out to Alumni

The alumni strategy is covered extensively in my first book. My message here is simple: reaching out to alumni working in fields or industries or companies you want to learn more about is vastly under-utilized. Alumni simply don't get asked. The alumni strategy can open doors if you are 21 or 51. Shared experience can open doors like no other.

Here are two different templates. The first is for a recent college graduate and the other for a more experienced professional.

Subject: Big U graduate hoping to connect

Hi Tommy,

Nice to virtually meet you! My name is Walter Sobchak, and I am a graduate of Big U, class of 2021. I am based here in Chicago now following my first job out of college. I've spent the past 2.5 years doing tech sales at XYZ, but I'm looking to make a transition into sports marketing.

While I was going through my job search, I came across your information, and I wanted to reach out. You've been very successful within XYZ, and I was hoping to grab 30 minutes with you either for a coffee in the city or over the phone to pick your brain about the industry and my best way to get my foot in the door with potential employers.

I have some questions, listed below, that I want to discuss. Please let me know if you have any availability over the coming week as it would be great to make and introduction and learn about your perspective.

- Is your work more team-oriented or individual oriented?

- What are the measurements for success?

- What are the nuances and differences in working in ____ that might be different than what I've done within tech?

- How have you transitioned from one role to the next in your career, and what were you trying to accomplish at each level?

- How does the day-to-day work influence long-term goals?

Thank you again for taking consideration in talking with me, and I look forward to connecting shortly!

Thank you,

Walter Sobchak

Here is a template for a more experience professional.

Subject: XYZ graduate hoping to connect

Hi, Joe,

My name is Scott Fitzgerald, and like you, I am a graduate of XYZ— 2018. I am in the early stages of considering a career change and am exploring different organizations.

I see you have been with XXX for over 12 years, and that is one of the organizations I would like to learn more about. I would certainly

Searching For A Job Sucks!

appreciate the opportunity to meet briefly over coffee—live or virtual —and ask some questions.

For example:

- *What attracted you to XXX in the first place and what has kept you there?*

- *How do you expect XXX to grow in the future?*

- *How do you see the company evolving its business as technology changes?*

- *What can you tell me about the culture and values—and how those are carried forth throughout the organization?*

- *What types of people are most successful at XXX?*

- *What makes the leadership team effective?*

In return, I am happy to share all I can about changes in the ABC industry if you are interested.

Let me know your schedule for the next couple of weeks so I can buy you coffee. I will do my best to work around your schedule.

Thanks so much,

Scott

As you can see in both emails, which can also be LinkedIn messages, the focus is on learning and getting smarter about your job search. Of course, everyone who agrees to meet understands the underlying goal is to find a job so don't feel disingenuous. Keep focused on your purpose and building strong relationships.

Reach Out to Companies Where You Would Like to Work

Another active strategy is to reach out to companies where you'd like to work. Ideally, you can find a connection who knows someone who works there or used to work there. Perhaps you can leverage the alumni strategy to make a connection. Otherwise, you will need to go in cold. The odds of success are not very high, but it's better than being one of 500 or more applying for the same job online. Look for organizations that are growing and hiring. If the right person sees your resume and falls in love with your background, and they have an immediate or near-term need, you may hear from someone.

Here is an example of an email message from an experienced professional:

Subject: Sales Director with a great track record

Hello, Dwight,

I hope this message finds you well. My name is Jim Hallpern, and I currently serve as the Director of Sales at Dunder Mifflin, a prominent leader in the regional office supplies industry. With over a decade of experience in sales management, I've consistently surpassed quotas, with only one exception, throughout my career.

I'm reaching out to you today because I'm contemplating a potential transition into the human resources and payroll industry. I believe your insights could greatly benefit me in this regard. I would be

Searching For A Job Sucks!

grateful for just thirty minutes of your time to ask some questions and gain a deeper understanding of this industry.

I'm flexible and willing to accommodate your schedule for a face-to-face meeting at your convenience. In return for your time and expertise, I would gladly offer insights into successful recruitment strategies for entry-level sales representatives at Dunder Mifflin. While I can't disclose anything proprietary, I'm more than happy to share valuable lessons we've learned along the way.

Thank you in advance for considering my request, Dwight. I look forward to speaking.

Best regards,

Jim Hallpern

Here is an example from a more recent college graduate:

Subject: Recent WXYZ grad looking to connect

Hi, Sam,

I hope this message finds you well. My name is Diane Chambers, and I recently graduated from WXYZ University with a BS in Business, specializing in accounting and finance.

As I embark on my career journey, I find myself considering various paths, one of which is a role in high-tech sales. Based on feedback from professors and friends, it seems my personality, stamina and persistence align well with the demands of a sales role. With this in mind, I'm eager to gain a deeper understanding of the day-to-day experiences of a professional salesperson.

CHAPTER 6: PUTTING IT ALTOGETHER - The Job Search Game Plan

I greatly would appreciate just thirty minutes of your time to ask questions that will provide insights into the intricacies of a career in sales. I'm flexible and more than willing to accommodate your schedule, whether that means meeting in person or virtually via Zoom. Additionally, if you're interested, I'd be happy to introduce you to someone with the WXYZ business school who may be able to assist you in connecting with recent graduates. Depending on your needs, I may also be able to provide some referrals.

Thank you for considering my request, Sam. I'm eagerly looking forward to the opportunity to connect and learn from your experiences.

Warm regards,

Diane Chambers

As I stated, this is a long shot, but you only need to hear back from one person to get the process started.

The entire purpose behind the game plan is to help people spend their time in the right places.

While not scientific, I think the following makes sense:

Networking—70%

Search firms—20%

Job boards—10%

Searching For A Job Sucks!

For most professionals, networking is where you will find the greatest success. When you think about it, it's also where you have the most control.

Interviewing and Offer

This has already been covered this extensively earlier in the book. Getting a job interview and a job offer is what this work is all about.

One question I often get asked is how many active opportunities I should have in play at any one time. My answer is as many as possible. You never know how long a search will take or which ones will result in an offer. Play the field for as long as you can and don't make a decision until you are forced to make one. Let the other competing organizations know you have other opportunities in play, but of course, their opportunity, based on what you know, is the most appealing. This will often motivate an organization to move its process along faster. This isn't a commitment to saying "yes" if offered a job. It's just an honest expression of your interest level. As you learn more, and you mostly likely will, your opinion may change. If you are dealing with a recruiter, external or internal, never forget their motivation is to make the placement. As much as you think they like you and you have found a friend for life, rely on yourself and others who know you well to help you make this very difficult call.

Friday

I like to leave Friday open so you can make up for what you may have missed during the week. If you were busy preparing for an interview, if you were interviewing for a job, or doing other tasks related to your job search, you will need this time to make up for the networking time you may have missed. Otherwise, Friday can be spent making connections and hopefully having conversations. This is also a good time to reflect on the week and to ask yourself three questions related to your job search:

- What should I stop doing because it doesn't seem to be working?

- What should I start doing that I have omitted from my process?

- What should I continue doing because it's generating results?

You want to be thoughtful in your approach and learn at every step along the way. There are many variables associated with your job search, so you often have to discover what makes sense to stop, start, and continue. That's the reason I have included stories from former job seekers in the book. Each one has a story to tell and lesson that can be learned that may apply to your own circumstances.

Saturday and Sunday

As anxious as you may feel about finding a new job, you need to take a break from your job search. Spend time with family, friends, have some fun and try to forget about the challenges associated with your job search. The mental break will recharge your batteries while your subconscious discovers new and creative approaches you haven't considered.

Searching For A Job Sucks!

Landing

As I have already stated, just when you thought you were done, there is more to do. As a separate step in the process, you need to say thank you to the people who have been generous with their time and resources and who deserve to be recognized. I want to draw attention to how important it is to show appreciation and to leave a positive, lasting impression on everyone you meet. There is no better way to do that than to say thank you. I am always shocked at how often this step in the process is skipped. The people who helped you along the way will want to know where you landed. They will also feel good knowing they made some difference. This is also an opportunity to offer your assistance wherever and whenever needed. This is how you pay it forward.

This is also the time to engage with your My Vital Few™ so you never have to search for a job again. While everyone deserves to be thanked, some people were more helpful than others. And, in some cases, you have formed a close bond you want to maintain. Now that you have identified your My Vital Few™ connections, all you need is a commitment to engage in Step 2—following up.

Summary

The Job Search Game Plan takes persistence, resilience, and a commitment to the process.

My hope is that you never have to go beyond Step 1. If you are like most, you will need the entire roadmap to achieve your desired outcome.

If you are currently working and busy, it will take time to work through the entire process. The only place to start is at the beginning. Go as far as you can while continually cycling back to Step 1 to do the necessary follow-up.

If you are unemployed, by definition, you will have more time. You will utilize the entire process, and hopefully, be regularly engaged in conversations that lead to further conversations, and eventually, lead to that ideal opportunity at the end of tunnel.

Lessons from a Job Seeker

Don't Take This Trip Alone

Jerry is 64 years old and has spent his entire career as an individual contributor doing business and software analysis and implementation. He recently accepted a position as a teacher where he will impart information technology (IT) to high school students.

Jerry had been laid off and was engaged in an eight-month job search looking for an IT role. With lots of IT layoffs occurring at this time, his search was particularly difficult. He also believes he experienced a fair amount of age bias.

He eventually started to look at other opportunities where he could use the same skills but in a different capacity. Once he made this decision, the opportunity to become a teacher happened very quickly. Jerry is excited to stay in the same field while helping young people learn about opportunities in IT. He hopes he can teach them skills and knowledge they can use beyond high school. He is looking

Searching For A Job Sucks!

forward to helping this rising generation make critical career decisions with the information he can share.

John found his search challenging because of the large number of people applying for each position. He would apply for a job one day and see 200 or more applications for the same job the very next day. He knew he was in a highly competitive job market.

What Jerry found most frustrating was his interaction with recruiters. Internal and external recruiters alike would tell him he had a great background and was the perfect fit for the job. After that: crickets. He would never hear anything back, which is code for ghosting. When he reached out for an update, if he was lucky to get a return call, he would find out they went in another direction, and he never knew why.

Most challenging was the impact on his self-worth and self-confidence. For many people, their identity is tied to their job and that all came crashing down for Jerry. The longer you remain unemployed and face rejection, the more you begin to question yourself, and the self-doubt you experience can be paralyzing.

What helped Jerry was having someone in a mentoring relationship to provide encouragement, advice, and support. He also had to make the decision to persevere and believe that something positive would eventually come along.

Ultimately, Jerry learned that it wasn't about him. He had to accept and embrace his skills and background and realize that many qualified people were applying for the same positions. For Jerry, it was a matter of waiting for the right opportunity to come along. He reminded himself he needed to be patient and open to different possibilities that he hadn't previously considered. For Jerry, it reminded him of the phrase, "let go and let God." He knew something good would eventually happen and needed to trust God to make it happen. Jerry's faith helped to sustain him throughout the process.

Jerry had previously applied for a job teaching middle school students, which he didn't get but he was now in the county application system. Out of the blue, he received a call from a high school principal looking for someone with Jerry's technical background to teach high school students IT. The principal was impressed with Jerry's IT knowledge, and his work and life experience were strong enough to make up for any teaching deficiencies.

If he had to do his job search over, Jerry would do more networking than he did. Getting in touch with friends, former colleagues, and so on was very helpful, but he wishes he had done more earlier in the search. Jerry is committed to staying in touch with those folks who helped him during his job search so he can hopefully pay it forward. He learned firsthand how much you need the support and assistance from others to find that ideal opportunity.

Before the school principal reached out to him, Jerry put a posting on LinkedIn describing his background and what he wanted to do next in his career. He learned through the process that the more you use LinkedIn or something like that to put yourself out there, the more visibility you can create. Jerry heard from a few folks offering to assist and he learned being a little vulnerable pays off. Even making a comment on a post keeps you in front of people.

Searching For A Job Sucks!

Jerry believes this opportunity to become a teacher is exactly what he is supposed to be doing and doesn't have the kind of nervousness you often have when you start a new job. He sees this as a great fit personally and professionally and can't wait to get started. Jerry has received lots of support and encouragement from friends and former colleagues, which has given his confidence a huge boost and makes him feel great!

As a follow-up to our initial interview, Jerry recently passed his PRAXIS exam that measures the skills and content knowledge you need to enter the classroom. He did this without ever studying or preparing to become a teacher. Sometimes you just know when it's right.

CHAPTER 7: FINAL THOUGHTS

You can't write a book about searching for a job without discussing technology. The artificial intelligence (AI) transformation in recruiting and hiring may be the most significant shift we've seen since the internet and the introduction of online job boards. For today's job seeker, the use of AI makes generating a resume, searching for a job and preparing for an interview easier than ever. What we see happening in the AI is both exciting and remarkable, and we are only at the beginning of what's possible.

I was recently asked by a colleague if we'll ever get to the point where candidates are interviewed by a machine programmed with AI. I could tell by the way he asked the question that he wasn't excited about the possibility. Unfortunately, I had to break the news to him: that day has arrived! Like I said, we haven't seen anything yet.

While I believe it is essential for job seekers to understand how AI can enable their job search, it may be more important for job seekers to understand how employers will use AI. Getting your foot in the door is only going to get harder.

A 2023 University of Southern California Annenberg article, titled "How Artificial Intelligence (AI) in HR Is Changing Hiring" cites data technology news provider Dataconomy and lists three core improvements to recruiting:

Searching For A Job Sucks!

1. How human resources (HR) reps are now able to sort through several resumes at a time using automated tools, saving the countless hours of manual scanning

2. How HR reps are now able to find the right candidates more quickly because AI tools are programmed to hone in on certain keywords and phrases

3. The ability of AI to be programmed to have no opinion on candidates' gender, race, or age so there's less chance of personal bias affecting recruiting

The article concludes that AI "does allow HR reps to do their jobs much more quickly and efficiently. For qualified job candidates, this means they can expect to hear back sooner. For hiring companies, it means filling vacancies more quickly."

In its report "The Future of Recruiting 2023," LinkedIn listed the recruiting outcomes hiring pros hope to see from generative AI.

> 74%—Automate repetitive task to prioritize more strategic work
>
> 67%—Make it faster/easier to source candidates
>
> 59%—Make it faster/easier to engage candidates

What both of these articles, and many others like them have in common is AI's ability to make recruiting and hiring more efficient. This is code for better ways to screen out people and reduce the amount of time speaking with candidates. If you were hoping for more human interaction in the recruiting and hiring process, I believe

CHAPTER 7: FINAL THOUGHTS

you are about to see even less. A lot of the work performed by recruiters will be performed by machines, with AI, that make many decisions before a human ever sees your resume. The focus will be on increasing productivity and cost cutting.

You can almost envision a world, in the not-too-distant future, where hiring managers are responding to recommendations made by automated assistants and only make a final decision. Who knows? We may reach a day when hiring decisions for some jobs are completely made via automation. That may sound extreme, but I say it to make a point.

All of this is another way to say that no one really cares about your experience as a candidate. HR will talk about the employee experience ad nauseam, and people will nod politely in agreement, but unfortunately, it's just a lot of talk.

So, What Do You Do?

It is important for you, as a job seeker, to understand everything you can about generative AI to help with your search. With everything changing so rapidly, it seems silly to go into specifics because everything I write will be outdated by the time you read this text. My strong recommendation is to dive into your favorite search engine and find the latest and greatest resources that are available and learn how they can help you.

Some of the questions you want to ask yourself include the following:

- How can AI clarify my direction?

Searching For A Job Sucks!

- How can AI help me generate email introductions?

- How can AI help me with a networking campaign?

- How can AI help me prepare for interviews?

- How can AI help me more easily stay in touch with people after I land?

I have two words of caution.

First, never let technology do all the work for you. It can clarify, fine-tune, and polish what you have created, but the final product needs to be your voice and your experience. This is especially true when writing a resume. You have to know and understand what you claim to be your work history. If you don't understand what is written or if it isn't 100% true, you will be in big trouble when it comes time to interview.

Second, in my "pre-Skynet Terminator" lifetime, I believe there is one reality about the hiring and recruiting process that I can't see changing. Hiring is still a face-to-face interaction that relies on a personal connection. Chemistry, fit, or whatever you call it still factors into the hiring process and it's hard to imagine that going away. Although in the spirit of efficiency or some other ridiculous reason, I'm sure we'll try.

Always remember that at the other end of an AI-generated email, or the compelling AI-generated job description, or the AI-generated interviewing questions is a living, breathing, person who is desperate to fill a job. Assuming you have the technical chops to perform the role, the final hiring decision will largely depend on the connection you establish and the relationship you begin building with the hiring manager.

A 2015 article in *Forbes,* titled "The No. 1 Predictor of Career Success According to Network Science," was about Steve Jobs and what led to his amazing success. The article stated: "According to multiple, peer-reviewed studies, simply being in an open network instead of a closed one is the best predictor of career success." The study noted that a closed network means you hear the same ideas over and over, which "reaffirm what you already believe. In an open network, you are exposed to new ideas." It concluded that "half of the predicted differences in career success (i.e., promotion, compensation, industry recognition) is due to this one variable: an open network."

The message is simple: focus on building, maintaining, and nurturing relationships throughout your career. Don't wait until you're laid off or in urgent need of a job. While AI is fascinating, avoid getting sidetracked by the latest trends. The importance of building strong relationships and rich networks is unlikely to ever change.

Searching For A Job Sucks!

ABOUT THE AUTHOR

Bill is the Co-founder and CEO of FitzDrake Search, Inc., an executive search and recruiting firm located in Northern Virginia. FitzDrake has been in business since 2004 and works with companies as large as the Fortune 500 to start-ups where he and his team place exceptional executive and professional-level talent.

Prior to owning his own firm, Bill worked at AOL, Hewlett Packard, and ADP. Bill has assisted thousands of job seekers and provides practical advice and actionable recommendations. He has published over 60 LinkedIn articles on leadership, the job search and career management.

Bill has an MSOD from Pepperdine University, an MS, Ed. S from SUNY Albany and a BA from SUNY Geneseo.

Bill is a best-selling author who published his first book, How to Find a New Job Without Looking, in April 2023.

Bill lives with his wife, Mary, and Jack the dog in Ashburn, Virginia. Bill and Mary have two grown daughters and a son-in-law living in the area.

Searching For A Job Sucks!

REFERENCES

7 counteroffer statistics every recruiter needs to know. (2018, January 23). Eclipse Software Marketing. https://shorturl.at/WlLMs

Akins, Kingsley. (n.d.). The Networking Institute. https://thenetworkinginstitute.com

Alabi, Tolu. (2023, January 30). *Why networking is important [+ How to get it right]*. HubSpot. https://shorturl.at/t6ZeH

Alt, Ashley. (n.d.). *Quiz: 4 questions to find your ikigai*. InHerSight. https://shorturl.at/WdzTb

Aragão, Carolina. (2023, March 1). *Gender pay gap in U.S. hasn't changed much in two decades*. Pew Research Center. https://shorturl.at/PstrM

Augustine, Amanda. (2021, December 14). *7 signs your resume is making you look old*. TopResume. https://shorturl.at/2EZbz

Batinovic, Lucija, Howe, Marion, Sinclair, Samantha, & Carlsson, Rickard. (2023, August 11). *Ageism in hiring: A systematic review and meta-analysis of age discrimination*. Collabra: Psychology. University of California Press. https://bit.ly/4gaU6qM

Borchers, Callum, & Ellis, Lindsay. (2024, May 30). *Landing a job is all about who you know (again)*. Wall Street Journal. https://on.wsj.com/49C8J3H

Bradshaw, Ryan. (2024, June 24). *15 important networking statistics everyone should know*. Apollo Technica—Engineered Talent Solutions. https://bit.ly/4ghmQ11

Brandon, Emily. (2020, April 27). *7 tips for getting hired after age 50*. US News & World Report. https://yhoo.it/4gxizpT

Can California employers ask job applicants salary history? (n.d.). Shouse California Law Group. https://bit.ly/3D5TZxV

Searching For A Job Sucks!

Carson, Richard David. (2003, July 8). *Taming your gremlin: A surprisingly simple method for getting out of your own way*. HarperCollins. https://shorturl.at/d485n

Castrillon, Caroline. (2024, September 22). *10 questions to ask a recruiter during a job interview*. Forbes. https://bit.ly/4iwVDZE

Caudron, Shari. (2002, August 9). *Why job applicants hate HR*. Workforce.com. https://bit.ly/3ZBxWad

Chamorro-Premuzic, Tomas. (2021, May 26). *The problem with job interviews*. Forbes. https://bit.ly/3OQ9hK3

Chan, Goldie. (2024, May 20). *Top careers based on your Myers-Briggs Personality Type*. Forbes. https://shorturl.at/LIkgb

Choi-Allum, Lona. (2022, July). *Age discrimination among workers age 50-plus*. Washington, DC: AARP Research. https://doi.org/10.26419/res.00545.001

Cox, Lindsay Kolowich. (n.d.). *21 things recruiters absolutely hate about your resume*. HubSpot. https://bit.ly/4fw5Rah

Danao, Monique. (2024, April 28). *11 essential soft skills in 2024 (with examples)*. Forbes. https://bit.ly/3Zx4QIQ

Dizikes, Peter. (2022, September 15). *The power of weak ties in gaining new employment*. MIT News. https://bit.ly/4iAQ4te

Elmers, Danielle. (2024, July 30). *The job-search statistics all job seekers should know*. TopResume. https://shorturl.at/ubqLB

Eren, Slecuk, & Hunter, Lisa. (2023, September 21). *2024 salary increase budgets stay elevated*. The Conference Board. https://shorturl.at/wbciM

Every executive search firm, recruiter or headhunter, anywhere in the USA. Recruit. https://bit.ly/3ORqaDV

References

Fennell, Andrew. (2022, November). *How long do recruiters spend looking at your resume?* StandOut CV. https://bit.ly/4gr1QoR

Fitzgerald, Bill. (2023, April 11). *How to find a new job without looking: Building vital relationships that lead to a successful career.* Amazon. https://shorturl.at/RT7Vn

Gaylor, Lila. (n.d.). *The salary history ban: 5 steps to determine pay in the don't-ask era.* Insperity. https://bit.ly/49yqp0m

Gilpin, Rachael. (2023, May 30). *Is LinkedIn Premium worth it? An in-depth guide for job seekers.* Teal. https://bit.ly/3Dc6jNb

Grainger, Charlotte. (n.d.). *How to respond to a recruiter on LinkedIn: 5 professional examples.* resume.io. https://bit.ly/3ZQnD3m

How artificial intelligence (AI) in HR is changing hiring. (2023, November 15). USC Annenberg. https://bit.ly/49Hd31W

How to respond to a recruiter on LinkedIn (with examples). (2024, July 17). Alijobs.ai https://bit.ly/4iuYTF5

Hunter. (n.d.). https://hunter.io/

Hyken, Shep. (2023, July, 9). *Beyond money: The real reasons employees stay or leave.* Forbes. https://bit.ly/41qdwn0

Interview Preparation Tool. LinkedIn. https://bit.ly/3VAPS3A

Iqbal, Mansoor. (2024, April 2024). *LinkedIn usage and revenue statistics (2024).* Business of Apps. https://bit.ly/41rM603

Jacquez, Katie. (2022, December 9). *I'm a designer at LinkedIn.* Medium. https://bit.ly/41sx3mR

Lyons, Marlo. (2022, February 9). *Do you need a career coach?* Harvard Business Review. https://bit.ly/3ZyIWoL

Searching For A Job Sucks!

Mbombera, Nomore. (2024, April 2). *41 reasons why job seekers hate HR professionals*. LinkedIn. https://bit.ly/3ZwrW2q

Mishel, Lawrence, & Kandra, Jori. (2021, August 10). *CEO pay has skyrocketed 1,322% since 1978*. Economic Policy Institute. https://bit.ly/3ZNxUNw

Nonprofit recruiters. (n.d.). Recruit. https://bit.ly/3BuvDxt

Peachman, Rachel Rabkin. (2024, May 7). *America's best executive recruiting firms*. Forbes. https://bit.ly/49BFnTp

People at Heart. Find your ikigai. Clarify your life purpose with this questionnaire and powerful exercise. https://bit.ly/4gxvjNj

Perna, Mark C. (2023, June 13). *5 marks of a toxic work culture—And how you know it's time to leave*. Forbes. https://bit.ly/4ir5Uqx

Richards, Elle. (2023, September 18). *10 things to check before accepting a job offer*. Vault. https://bit.ly/3DeVOJa

Salary history bans. (2024, May 8). HRDIVE. https://bit.ly/3VDehFr

Samir, Chaymae. (2024. August 27). *How to find a headhunter or recruiter to get you a job now*. Zety. https://bit.ly/41vD9CY

Schein, Edgar. (n.d.) MIT Management Career Development Office. https://bit.ly/3ZR9Ppk

Schifeling, Jeremy. (2023. June 21). *Expensive career coach*. GBT. https://bit.ly/4gxvA2N

Simmons, Michael. (2015, January 15). *The No. 1 predictor of career success according to network science*. Forbes. https://bit.ly/4go7M1u

Sull, Donald, Sull, Charles, & Zweig, Ben. (2022, January 11). *Toxic culture is driving the Great Resignation*. MIT Sloan Management Review. https://bit.ly/4f9H5fK

References

Sumser, John. (n.d.). *The odds of getting a job with a recruiter*. *HR Examiner*. https://bit.ly/3OTkfOF

Survey: 2023 US salary increase budgets reach 22-year high. (2023. October, 17). Conference Board Press Release. https://bit.ly/3DmpSCq

Tayal, Raghav. (2023, February 10). *9 ways to find anyone's email address in 2024 (tried and tested)*. Digital Web Solutions. https://bit.ly/4irakxz

Tegze, Jan. (2017, July 14). *The 7 reasons why people change jobs*. RecruitingDaily. https://bit.ly/3OUNaC6

The future of recruiting 2023. (n.d.). LinkedIn. https://bit.ly/3OVMoVv

The truth about counteroffers from a recruiter's perspective. (n.d.). Progressive. https://bit.ly/3ZM7DiF

Tieger, Paul D., Barron, Barbara, & Tieger, Kelly. (2021). *Do what you are: Discover the perfect career for you through the secrets of personality type*, 5th ed. New York: Hachette Book Group. https://amzn.to/3ZyuIEb

Want to nail an interview? Use mirroring. (2013, May). Forbes. https://bit.ly/4ivDA6e

Washle, Kiersten, & Deborah, Lenny. (2024). *The importance of networking*. Journal of Energy Management. https://bit.ly/3ZOzUoF

When should you take a pay cut? (2023, August 28). System|One. https://bit.ly/3VCRY2C

Why you should never accept a counteroffer. (May 12). Redshift. https://bit.ly/3DcVYRe

Williams, Chris. (2024, February 26). *How long is too long at one job? How short is too short? Microsoft's ex-VP of HR explains*. Business Insider. https://bit.ly/4g9kK3m

Zagami, Brennan. (2023, March 29). *Study finds that nearly one-third of job postings are fake*. COMPXL. https://bit.ly/3ZwDeDS

www.ingramcontent.com/pod-product-compliance
Lightning Source LLC
Chambersburg PA
CBHW020628220526
45464CB00001B/65